IT'S ABOUT
TIME

IT'S ABOUT TIME

THE ART OF CHOOSING
THE MEANINGFUL OVER THE URGENT

VALORIE BURTON

W Publishing Group

AN IMPRINT OF THOMAS NELSON

Published in Nashville, Tennessee, by W Publishing, an imprint of Thomas Nelson.

The author is represented by Alive Literary Agency, 7680 Goddard Street, Suite 200, Colorado Springs, Colorado 80920, www.aliveliterary.com.

Thomas Nelson titles may be purchased in bulk for educational, business, fund-raising, or sales promotional use. For information, please e-mail SpecialMarkets@ThomasNelson.com.

Any Internet addresses, phone numbers, or company or product information printed in this book are offered as a resource and are not intended in any way to be or to imply an endorsement by Thomas Nelson, nor does Thomas Nelson vouch for the existence, content, or services of these sites, phone numbers, companies, or products beyond the life of this book.

Unless otherwise indicated, Scripture quotations are taken from the Holy Bible, New International Version®, NIV®. Copyright © 1973, 1978, 1984, 2011 by Biblica, Inc.™ Used by permission of Zondervan. All rights reserved worldwide. www.zondervan.com. The "NIV" and "New International Version" are trademarks registered in the United States Patent and Trademark Office by Biblica, Inc.™

ISBN 978-0-7852-2011-4 (eBook)
ISBN 978-0-7852-2018-3 (TP)

Library of Congress Cataloging-in-Publication Data

Library of Congress Control Number: 2018915210

Printed in the United States of America

19 20 21 22 23   LSC   10 9 8 7 6 5 4 3 2 1

To my husband, Jeff.
You jumped into this "experiment" with time without
hesitation. And the journey that has unfolded as a result is
beyond anything I had imagined. Thank you. I love you.

CONTENTS

THIS IS WHERE
I STARTED

The subject of time is something I have wrestled with my entire life. I've always seemed to think I can get more done in a day than I can, leaving me with the feeling that I've never done enough. I've jokingly called myself a "recovering procrastinator," and the modern pull of digital distractions has made it easier than ever to put off the things that matter. Not to mention, my struggle with perfectionism has meant it's never quite the right time to get started anyway. Then I found myself racing against a biological clock in my thirties, afraid my life's most meaningful dream might pass me by altogether. Because my struggle with time has often felt like a stronghold, a thorn in my side I could not pluck out, I have desperately wanted to untangle its grip on my life. The day it came to me that I should write this book was pretty frustrating. I will share more about that in a moment, but let me encourage you that sometimes it is your frustration that fuels your turnaround. Sometimes you become so exasperated by the thought of continuing on the path you have been traveling that you suddenly feel the conviction to finally do whatever it takes to change. That is the place where this journey started. For years, I coached others to get unstuck, and now I needed to get myself unstuck.

I invite you to step through this journey with me, as I share time-less truths and practical steps that will open your eyes to the insidious nature of our problem with time. It is a problem that has evolved, slowly taking us further and further from nature's rhythm and moving us toward the unsustainable pace and load of a technology age. You, me, and millions of others struggle daily to keep up.

I knew deep down that the journey I embarked on was not just for me. It was meant to make its way onto the page to help you too. That thought was intimidating, but also motivating. The pressure and accountability of helping you ultimately helped me. My desire is for you to walk away from this book with an understanding of the eternal value of your finite time—and why and how you must intentionally choose the meaningful over the urgent every single day.

Our culture makes it so that even the most organized and efficient among us feels the pressure of the ticking clock and the possibility and regret of missing out. Modern life has evolved in a way that sets us up for stress, pressure, and overload. New norms and attitudes tap into deeply wired psychological impulses that make it harder than ever to take control of our time. Many of us also have one or more innate personality traits that make the struggle even worse. Perhaps you can relate to one or more of them:

- Optimism
- Perfectionism
- Overachieving
- Over-responsibility
- Approval addiction
- Misplaced guilt

No wonder time can become a tyrant that leaves you chronically stressed and discontented.

It would be enough if the ultimate consequences were only stress and discontentment. But those are just symptoms. Instead, it's the prospect of living a life in which you spend your time doing the things that *seem* important, only to look back and realize you missed out on the things that actually *are*. Today, this ultimate consequence is becoming the fate of more and more people. The natural pace and rhythm of life has been disrupted and replaced by historical and cultural shifts I will describe in the coming chapters—shifts that have created new habits that have become so common they are the new normal. These shifts make it easy to choose the things that feel normal (because everyone else is doing them) over the things that are natural (because they grow out of how you were created to function).

My guess is you chose this book because something about the title, the cover, or the description resonated with you. Or perhaps someone gave it to you because they sensed you need it. Whatever led you here, you will discover the ways in which the world has redefined what is normal and gain an understanding of how that personally impacts you daily. My hope is that you broaden your perspective and see your life in the greater context of our increasingly demanding world. I will help you reimagine the possibilities for a life that is meaningful, at a pace that is natural, with a load that is doable. Then I will equip you with the tools to bring that meaningful life to fruition.

Through these pages we will explore three key pieces of information that will help you unlock an approach to life that I call *living timelessly*:

1. The history and gradual changes that have led us to a place where having too much to do and too little time to do it is the norm
2. The vision for what it could be like if you were free from the stress of time and understood the obstacles you must blast through to enjoy the life you long for
3. The practical steps to choosing the meaningful over the

urgent so that your life is unhurried yet purposeful, and
reflects the values and the impact you want to make that are
unique to you

BREAKING FREE OF OLD
HABITS IN A NEW SEASON

My professional journey has been a long road. I self-published my
first book after discovering my life purpose in 1999. I was clear. I was
inspired. And I was determined to follow the purpose I knew in my
spirit I was made for:

*To create and enjoy a fulfilling, prosperous, and charitable life—and
to inspire others to do the same.*

I remember so clearly the day I stood in the "women's interest"
book section of a Barnes & Noble bookstore during a trip to Seattle
and had a flash of inspiration about that purpose. I remember writing that mission statement and staring at it as I sat in bed journaling
in my little condo in Dallas, where I lived at the time. I remember
the possibilities that danced through my imagination, filling me with
hope and energy for my future. And I remember the quiet intensity of
writing my first book in cursive on legal notepads, too intimidated by
the blank computer screen to type it all out. I felt so connected to those
words, as if they were coming to me and then through me. Sitting at
the desk in my spare bedroom on weekends and weeknights, I wrote
my career into existence and dreamed that it could one day become
all that I hoped.

My life today is so much of what I had hoped for. Like you, I have
fought to get where I am. And yet I believe there is so much more
to come.

In order to pursue my purpose years ago, I learned to do a lot
with very little. Because my previous career was in marketing and

public relations, I was able to use those skills to build and manage my business while simultaneously producing the content—books, media, coaching, and speaking—that is the essence of the business. For the first seven years, I bootstrapped it. And once I got my footing, I never stopped bootstrapping it. An abiding fear of not having enough has often driven me to be really conservative about my financial commitments yet overzealous about my time commitments. The habit of being conservative has served me well, as has the willingness to work hard, but like any good thing, too much of it can become bondage.

OUR LIVES ARE FULL

Like yours, my life is full. I am sometimes stretched thin by my travel schedule, three kids, and a husband who is a commercial pilot and travels fourteen-plus days per month. You have your own set of demands: your work, your commute, your children's needs, school, debt that compels you to earn as much money as possible, and striving to get to the "next level," whatever that looks like. The fact that living with no breathing room has become the norm for a large segment of the population is a threat to our well-being and happiness. There is an undeniable connection between time and happiness.

Perhaps you have so much to be grateful for, yet little time to enjoy it fully. Maybe you find yourself reaching milestones, only to push the finish line out just a little farther—always another project, another goal, another level. And perhaps you have started to wonder, *When have I done enough?* It is an unfamiliar question in an achievement-driven world—but it is a question that intrigues the soul of anyone who wants to be truly happy and create breathing room to enjoy the life she has created.

The journey to a life in which I am happily married, have the privilege of being a mom and a bonus mom, do work I truly love, and have strong friendships to cherish took many years. As it finally came together, I awakened to the reality that time and happiness are intricately interconnected. Margin empowers happiness. It is breathing room—the soft cushion between your schedule and your limits. And in today's world we have less of it than ever.

If you'll allow me, I will share throughout these pages a little of my personal journey, the fun experiments that helped me—along with my husband, Jeff—change our lives, and my hope for how they could help you change yours.

OUR AHA MOMENT

While I was stuck in the Phoenix airport for ten hours on a trip I wished I had said no to, I had an epiphany that became the catalyst for this book. I was sitting at a tiny little Mexican restaurant in the terminal with my good friend Yvette, who had traveled with me for a business event. While we were waiting for our food, I poured out my frustration to her.

"I've always crammed more into my schedule than is sane," I said, reflecting on my deeply ingrained habit. What I really wanted was some insight—an answer that could help me break the cycle. And Yvette, being the wise businesswoman and coach that she is, was just the person who might be able to deliver.

"When I think about it, I was always praised for doing things fast, being the first, the youngest," I pondered aloud. "I finished college at twenty, grad school at twenty-one, started a business at twenty-four, and wrote my first book by twenty-six. Getting to the finish line fast was my identity."

That's when Yvette posed a simple but profound question.

"And what has that gotten you?" she asked.

I took a deep breath and exhaled. I briefly revisited each of those seasons of my life as I contemplated what might be different had I not rushed through them but had instead traveled a little slower, savored a little longer.

My mind drew a blank on the answer to her question.

"What has it gotten me?" I repeated back to her. "I'm not sure it has gotten me much. Well, except more stress. I often missed out on the journey while I was trying to get to some self-imposed finish line. But the finish line was usually lonely, less exciting and not as happy as I'd imagined it would be." Overachievement had been such a driver for me because it indeed gave me something: approval and acceptance. That vulnerability led me to overcommit, and at times, overwork.

Have you ever had a moment where a thought so deeply resonated with you that you just had to sit with it to process it? This was one of those moments.

The cashier interrupted my thoughts when she called out that my food was ready. I went to the counter to get my quesadilla and then sat back down at the table with Yvette.

"I'm still that twentysomething young woman racing to a finish line that keeps getting pushed out. I have everything I thought I wanted in life—a loving, fun, supportive husband, children I feel uniquely called to raise, purposeful work, family within minutes from home. But I am doing too much. I want more time to savor it!" I lamented.

"Maybe your flight being delayed is a message," Yvette said with a chuckle. "You know God will sometimes stop us in our tracks to get our attention."

As if on cue, my phone started ringing. It was my husband, Jeff, FaceTiming to tell me he'd had an epiphany about our jam-packed lifestyle.

"You know how you're always talking about margin?" he asked, as though he'd been eavesdropping on the conversation.

"Yes," I said.

"I never really got what you were talking about," he admitted.

"But I was sitting here meditating, and it occurred to me that I don't think I've had margin for at least ten years!"

Stunned, I had to stop and wrap my head around the first part of that last sentence: *I was sitting here meditating.* Jeff's faith is at his core; however, when I had suggested he spend time in quiet meditation, he'd brushed me off. But recently he'd decided to try it, and lo and behold, he got clarity about margin on the same day I was wrestling with the same issue!

Whenever a great speaking opportunity came along, I'd ask him, "Do you think I should do this? I mean, do you think this is good for our schedules?" And without hesitation, he'd *always* answer the same way: "Do it. That sounds great." It's in his nature to be supportive of my career, so his answer was always yes. But I was asking his opinion because I realized our schedules were already full and I needed help saying no. So this call was a *big deal.* On this day, in the middle of the airport, he called to say he finally got it.

"I don't know what we need to do differently, but we need to do something," he declared. It was our aha moment.

EXPERIMENTING WITH CHANGE

Within a few weeks, we embarked on some experiments to see if we could get control of our time. Our goals were to create more meaningful experiences, make more time for each other and for our children, and decrease our stress. We called them "experiments" because we didn't want to make big declarations about what to change, only to discover we couldn't live up to them permanently or that they weren't having the impact we'd hoped for. Making these changes and activities into experiments felt doable, flexible, and, frankly, fun. If they worked, we'd keep them up. If they didn't, we could drop them or tweak them without feeling like we'd failed.

#MEANINGFULOVERURGENT

We began by simply talking about what we were feeling and what we wanted to feel instead. Summarizing how I felt was simple: I felt as though I were eating my favorite dessert, homemade strawberry cake, but I was being forced to eat it in record time with a stopwatch hovering over me, rather than savoring one piece at a time. In other words, my schedule had become so overloaded I couldn't enjoy the very things I love. Time with my husband and children always felt rushed or too short, and the work I am passionate about felt like an intrusion on my life. Jeff felt a lack of clarity about the impact of his schedule on our lives. For more than fourteen years, he's been a dad who flies an average of two weeks every month. When he's home, he's all here. But when gone, he's totally gone— sleeping in different cities nearly every night, wherever his last flight of the day happens to land.

So we each began with simple experiments. I reflected on my original life vision. I can still picture the day I pulled up to my apartment during my first semester of grad school in journalism. I had a flash of inspiration that day that I could have a family life and a professional life without climbing a corporate ladder if I used my writing gift to become an author. I didn't know what kind of author at the time, but with my lifelong passion for books, the thought excited me.

I had tucked that dream away all of these years, and now, as I pondered the idea of getting control of my time and happiness, the inspiration that came to me two decades ago returned. It dawned on me that I was living my vision, but I wasn't taking advantage of the purpose behind the vision: the flexibility to control my schedule. Instead, I was working as though I had to abide by a corporate work schedule—you know, the norm of an eight-to-five routine. But why? What was the point of being my own boss if my schedule didn't meet my needs and those of my family? So my first experiment was to create a new normal for my work schedule—one that gave me the breathing room I needed.

As a coach, I believe I find the best answers by asking powerful questions—or PQs, as I like to call them when I am training personal and executive coaches. PQs are one of my favorite coaching tools, and I'll share lots of them throughout this book. I started with this one: What if I didn't have to work every day in order to get my work done?

Just asking the question was inspiring. *What if I worked every* other *day?* I pondered. Hmm. That might feel like breathing room. I was intrigued but apprehensive. Could I get my work done? Would I feel guilty because my team was still working every day? Would it hurt my business? I decided I wouldn't know unless I tried it. I committed to doing it for thirty days. After thirty days, I realized my fears were unfounded, so I continued the every-other-day schedule for an entire year. Two surprising things happened as a result.

First, compared to when I worked every day, I was *more* productive, not less. This schedule forced me to prioritize, so I cut some activities that were not particularly meaningful for the goals of the business. I became more selective about what meetings I could attend because there was limited time for them. And I was much more focused during my work days because I knew I had to get my work done or I could not take the following day off. It was built-in accountability.

Second, and amazingly, during the year when I worked less than I ever had in twenty years of business, we had our highest revenues to date. Taking time off didn't hurt the business; it seemed to have helped it. Not only was I more focused, but I was also more creative and happier. Time away from the office helped me gain perspective and see the big picture. And my team took ownership of projects in new ways, generating ideas and solutions to problems without my input. It felt as if I'd hit the jackpot.

At the same time, we did an experiment for Jeff to gain the clarity he wanted about his schedule. One evening after the kids went to bed, we pulled out the flip chart we used for family meetings, calculated how he spent his time in a typical month, and created a visual that I call a time chart. He had a black marker in his hand and a calculator.

Ever since that day in the Phoenix airport, when he told me he hadn't had breathing room in his life since becoming a parent more than a decade ago, he'd said he needed to make a time chart. I wasn't sure what he meant by that, but as I sank into the sofa, eyes fixed on the numbers he was writing on the large white sheets of paper, suddenly I got it. Jeff wanted to figure out how he was spending his life—or rather, his time. And he didn't like what he saw.

He took the schedule for that month and broke it down by work, sleep, family time, marriage time, commute time, and more. And as he calculated the numbers, we were flabbergasted. Here's what we estimated based on 720 hours in a thirty-day month:

TIME EXPENSE	ESTIMATED AMOUNT OF TIME SPENT IN HOURS	PERCENT OF TIME USED (BASED ON 720-HOUR MONTH)
Working as a pilot 14 days per month (traveling, flying, sleeping away from home)	336+	47
Sleeping at home	128	18
Transporting the girls to school, appointments, and extracurricular activities	54	8
Eating with and cooking for the family	32	6
Personal hygiene on days at home	10	1

Whoa. We sat on the sofa and stared at the numbers. Seeing the hours written on the flip chart made three things clear. First, his work took up nearly half of his life. The average full-time person spends about 197 hours per week (27 percent of their time) on work, including getting ready for work and commuting. But as an airline captain, Jeff doesn't come home when he's working, so he spent 336 hours per month away for work. That was 47 percent of his available time each month.

Second, he hadn't realized how much time he spent driving. Jeff has joint custody of two kids from his previous marriage, and they attend school about thirty minutes from our home. The girls have a joke that they drive to Alaska each school year (we travel about seven thousand miles a year going to and from school). At the time, one was in elementary school and the other was in middle school, so that meant an hour-and-a-half round trip to take them to school in the morning and more than two hours to pick them up, since their schools let out an hour apart. Plus, on some days they had extracurricular activities. As a parent, you gladly do what you have to do to raise your children. But seeing the hours on paper was eye-opening.

Third, after calculating five basic activities, we realized Jeff had just 20 percent of his time left to do everything else in his life—from working out and running errands to time with me and our three children, not to mention time with friends or leisure time. It became obvious that something needed to change.

Just these two simple experiments opened the door to change. The benefit of using experiments to clarify how to take control of your time is not unique to me and my family. I believe if you are willing to map out your own journey by trying small changes and building on them, you will see transformation, perhaps in unexpected ways. In fact, I think that time charts are so revealing, I'm going to ask you to create your own, even before you read chapter 1. (See "This Is How You Start.")

After we began these experiments, we started asking questions of ourselves:

- What are our true priorities, and how does the way we spend our time reflect those priorities?
- What stresses us most about the time challenges we face, and what do we control that could ease that stress?
- Looking into the future, what is our hope for the big change we'd like to see for ourselves and our family?

Our answers to these questions led to more small experiments that ultimately brought about big and unexpected changes in our work and personal lives. Here are a few of our small experiments:

- Jeff and I took once-a-month "staycations" in which we cleared the calendar for the day and spent that time doing something we both enjoy—going for a hike, getting a massage, or doing absolutely nothing at all.
- We left our phones at the front door for the first two hours after arriving home, rather than keeping them on us in the house.
- We tried flying together as a family to some of my speaking engagements. Doing so meant that rather than being away from home, "home" came with me, alleviating the stress of being apart. This required doing something Jeff had never done in eighteen years of flying: dropping trips from his schedule. This meant earning less money and making budget adjustments.
- When Jeff's company offered its pilots the unique opportunity to go on hiatus for a month, we jumped at the chance. He had a full month off, and we got to experience what daily life feels like when one person is not working.

As we put these experiments into practice, some healthy changes followed. We went as a family to speaking engagements in Florida, Texas, Ohio, New York, Pennsylvania, and even South Africa. Jeff gave up his nightly glasses of wine to de-stress and chose instead to exercise and pursue his own spiritual growth. We researched the idea of non-traditional schooling options for our son. We started talking about our dreams because we had time to just talk. In other words, we naturally began moving toward conversations and decisions that were meaningful rather than dealing with only the seemingly urgent matters of racing through our overloaded schedules. Margin gave us time to think and room to dream. And that's when something unexpected happened.

One day, while I was on the internet, a listing for a home appeared. To this day, I don't know where it came from. I don't remember if it was a social media post or an ad. But when I saw it, it reminded me of a dream my husband had shared with me before we got married. He had mentioned it while we were house hunting, and I had chuckled because it was so unusual. He told me that someday he wanted a house with an airstrip because his dream was to have his own small airplane.

"A house with an airstrip?" I had retorted with a laugh. "Where do you think we're going to find that?"

"Oh, they have neighborhoods where people share an airstrip," Jeff explained matter-of-factly. And then he drove me by one of the neighborhoods. *Who knew?* I thought and tucked the idea in the back of my mind for someday . . . someday way down the road. *Maybe.*

When I saw that house, I thought of his faraway dream and emailed the listing to him—not because I was thinking of moving but because I thought it would be neat to share it.

Unbeknownst to me, my husband began driving by that house a couple of times a week, daydreaming about the possibilities. Not only did the property have a shared airstrip, but it was also a horse farm. He grew up with horses and had worked on his family's dairy farm during the summers. It was his dream to have that life as an adult.

About six weeks passed before we decided to take an official look at the property. We were both reluctant. We had a plan, and it did not involve moving to a farm and having horses. But within minutes of stepping onto it, I felt a sense of peace. I remembered my own dream as a young adult of living in the country—but not too far from a big city—and having horses and land. It was a dream I'd buried long ago. As unplanned and different as this was from our home in a cul-de-sac in a subdivision with hundreds of houses, something about this just felt right. And so we went for it.

The process of writing this book led to experiments that opened up breathing room, which helped us rediscover our long-forgotten dreams and bring them to life. What occurred as a result came as a complete surprise and was quite the opposite of how I expected this journey to unfold.

As you begin on this journey, perhaps you'll discover your own beautiful surprises. You've landed on these pages with a hope, but what you receive instead might just be better than you imagined.

THIS IS HOW
YOU START

I see you. I see you trying to skip past this section and go straight to chapter 1.

Don't do it.

Before you read any further, I want you to create your own time chart. Having this data in front of you will allow you to more easily identify problem areas and create experiments that can lead to long-term change.

Using the blank charts provided here or downloaded from valorieburton.com, write down the following:

- A list of your "time expenses," the activities that reflect how you spend your time
- The cost of each time expense in hours or minutes per day
- The cost of each time expense per week
- The cost of each time expense per month
- The percentage of time each time expense requires of your life

Be as accurate with your calculations as you can, and resist the temptation to judge yourself for the results. This is a tool to generate solutions, not cause shame or stress. Keep the chart handy as you read; it may help you answer the many questions I'll ask about how you spend your time.

Daily Time Chart

TIME EXPENSE	ESTIMATED AMOUNT OF TIME SPENT IN HOURS	PERCENT OF TIME USED (BASED ON 24-HOUR DAY)
Sleeping		
Eating		
Preparing for meals		
Commuting		
Exercising		
Working		
Traveling for work (not commuting)		
Getting kids ready for school/bed		
Doing homework (yours or your children's)		
Attending school		
Spending time as a household		
Maintaining personal hygiene		
Engaging in leisure time		
Driving family members/friends		
Grocery shopping		

Doing laundry		
Cleaning the house		
Socializing with friends		
Browsing social media		
Watching television/other screen viewing (includes internet time other than social media)		
Attending hair/nail appointments		
Engaging in self-care activities		
Participating in extracurricular activities (yours or your children's)		
Attending health appointments		
Dating/romantic activities		
Spending time with extended family		
Worshiping		

Total daily hours expended: _____

Balance: _____

Percent of time spent (daily hours expended divided by 24): _____

Weekly Time Chart

TIME EXPENSE	ESTIMATED AMOUNT OF TIME SPENT IN HOURS	PERCENT OF TIME USED (BASED ON 168-HOUR WEEK)
Sleeping		
Eating		
Preparing for meals		
Commuting		
Exercising		
Working		
Traveling for work (not commuting)		
Getting kids ready for school/bed		
Doing homework (yours or your children's)		
Attending school		
Spending time as a household		
Maintaining personal hygiene		
Engaging in leisure time		
Driving family members/friends		
Grocery shopping		
Doing laundry		
Cleaning the house		
Socializing with friends		

Browsing social media		
Watching television/other screen viewing (includes internet time other than social media)		
Attending hair/nail appointments		
Engaging in self-care activities		
Participating in extracurricular activities (yours or your children's)		
Attending health appointments		
Dating/romantic activities		
Spending time with extended family		
Worshiping		

Total weekly hours expended: _____

Balance: _____

Percent of time spent (weekly hours expended divided by 168): _____

Monthly Time Chart

TIME EXPENSE	ESTIMATED AMOUNT OF TIME SPENT IN HOURS	PERCENT OF TIME USED (BASED ON 720-HOUR MONTH)
Sleeping		
Eating		
Preparing for meals		
Commuting		
Exercising		
Working		
Traveling for work (not commuting)		
Getting kids ready for school/bed		
Doing homework (yours or your children's)		
Attending school		
Spending time as a household		
Maintaining personal hygiene		
Engaging in leisure time		
Driving family members/friends		
Grocery shopping		
Doing laundry		
Cleaning the house		
Socializing with friends		

Browsing social media		
Watching television/other screen viewing (includes internet time other than social media)		
Attending hair/nail appointments		
Engaging in self-care activities		
Participating in extracurricular activities (yours or your children's)		
Attending health appointments		
Dating/romantic activities		
Spending time with extended family		
Worshiping		

Total monthly hours expended: _____

Balance: _____

Percent of time spent (monthly hours expended divided by 720): _____

CHAPTER ONE

THE NEW NORMAL
IS *NOT NORMAL*

The morning of her father's open-heart surgery, Marie had an ambitious plan to take her children to school, attend a work meeting, and get back in time to see her father before he went into surgery.

As a top-producing sales executive and divorced mom with sole custody of her three children, Marie was accustomed to juggling an overloaded schedule. Work had become her priority because, with no child support, she wanted to do everything she could to make sure her kids didn't suffer financially. It wasn't the way she had imagined her life when she was younger, but it was her reality, and she tried to make the best of it. Almost daily, she raced from one appointment to the next.

Marie is an optimist. It was part of what had gotten her promoted to vice president in an industry where such a position was rare for a woman. And her plan that Wednesday morning was nothing if not optimistic.

The previous day was like most others. Marie's father picked up the kids from school as he did every day and brought them to her house. When she arrived home, the kids were doing their homework, and her dad even had dinner on the stove. He was outside skimming the pool, a weekly chore he gladly did for her. But on this day, instead of standing over the pool with the skimmer and walking around the perimeter, he was sitting down. She stepped outside and asked him if he was okay. He said he was tired and felt like he had a little indigestion. She gave him some over-the-counter medicine, but when he didn't get any better, she became concerned. Her dad had been diagnosed with heart disease several years earlier and had a pacemaker, so if this wasn't indigestion, she was afraid it might be something much more serious. She picked up the phone and called 911.

She followed the ambulance to the hospital, where an EKG revealed he'd suffered a mild heart attack. The doctors insisted he have triple bypass heart surgery the very next day. Marie had an urgent meeting the next morning. Instinctively, she contemplated how she could go to both.

Her dad's surgery was at 10:00 a.m., and her office in downtown Dallas was just a twenty-minute drive from the hospital. So she came up with a game plan. The next morning, she would drop her two sons and daughter off at school by 7:30 a.m., attend the one-hour meeting that started at 8:00 a.m., then rush out as soon as it was over and arrive at the hospital by 9:30 a.m., just in time to tell her father she loved him and everything would be okay.

The meeting ran over by ten minutes, and she drove as fast as she could to the hospital. But by the time she arrived, it was 9:40 a.m., and her father had already been wheeled away for surgery. Marie was so disappointed.

What was I thinking? she berated herself as she reflected on her whirlwind morning.

Frustrated with herself for her decision, she headed into the surgery waiting room and sat with her mother and brother. It was a long few hours, but her father was eventually brought out of surgery and taken to the critical care unit (CCU) to recover. He had made it!

"The doctor said it took longer than expected, but he was doing well," she recalls. "A couple of the arteries were worse than originally thought. The doctor said as soon as they got him settled in his room, we could see him." They were all relieved.

Marie sat quietly as her mom and brother chatted with her mom's best friend, who'd joined them in the waiting room. She was thinking and people watching when she noticed something out of the corner of her eye.

"I saw lights flashing, and I heard the hospital activate a code blue," she remembers. It was a big hospital; the code blue could have been for any patient, but Marie felt led to walk to the door of the critical care unit out of curiosity. "I cannot tell you how, but I just knew it was him." As nurses and doctors rushed down the hall to the unknown patient, panic overwhelmed Marie. She prayed intensely, pleading with God to spare her father's life.

Within a few minutes, she saw the nurse who had taken care of her father the night before crying as she walked out of the CCU. "I didn't say anything to anyone," Marie says. "My mom, my brother, and my mom's best friend were still chatting. They hadn't noticed any of the activity going on outside of the waiting room."

Soon, though, they saw the distant gaze on Marie's face. They asked her what was wrong. Marie replied softly, "I think it's Dad."

While in recovery, he had gone into cardiac arrest. Determined to bring him back, the surgeon opened him up right there in the CCU and began massaging his heart by hand to get it beating again. But to no avail. Her father never regained consciousness. He was gone.

The nurse ushered them into the room for one last opportunity to see him after he passed. Marie says his lips were pressed together in a beautiful, ear-to-ear smile. "None of us cried in that moment," she recalls. "He was at peace."

But Marie was not. She was drenched with guilt and sadness—and deeply disappointed in herself. She had traded her last opportunity to see her father alive—to look him in the eyes and tell him how much he meant to her—for a sales meeting that could have gone on without her.

"I don't even remember what that 'urgent' 8:00 a.m. meeting was about or even who was in it!" Marie now says with deep regret. "What daughter would forgo seeing her dad before surgery for a meeting? It was my wake-up call."

Marie thought she could do it all. It was her norm—trying to do too much in too little time. Her overloaded lifestyle clouded her view of reality. So used to squeezing it all in, it never occurred to her that she couldn't—and shouldn't—attempt to go to both the sales meeting and her father's surgery. This is a consequence of a norm that is not natural. It is natural to choose the meaningful. It's what we crave. But when our lives are filled with too many commitments, we can't hear the craving of our souls for the meaningful over the false urgencies that demand our time.

Some decisions in life don't give us second chances to get it right. The sad truth is that we have to learn to live with a poor decision that cannot be undone. We can forgive ourselves—and if we are wise, we will take steps to make sure we don't find ourselves in the same predicament again.

In your day-to-day life, the stakes might not seem as high as missing the last opportunity to see a loved one alive. But who knows what tomorrow holds? If given the foresight to know it was the last day of her father's life, of course Marie would have made a different choice. We all would. But we don't get that privilege in life. We don't know which day will be a loved one's last—or ours.

We don't know how much stress will be too much stress on our bodies before we get that diagnosis. We don't know what the breaking point is in that relationship before the other person starts pulling away because they are tired of being so low on our priority list. We don't know when our children will give up hope of having a parent who is fully present and listens to them, and instead turn to dysfunctional ways to cope. Frankly, sometimes we don't know just how much the pace and load of life are stripping away the very essence of who we are—causing us to be irritable and demanding, stealing our creativity and joy, and making life more about *doing* than *being*.

Here's what we do know: if we intentionally choose what's meaningful over the false urgencies that try to demand our attention daily, then we can reclaim our time and live lives that we will look back on with peace rather than regret.

If I had a video recording of how you've spent your time over the past week, would it reflect the values and vision you say are priorities in your life? Or would you, like Marie, make some different choices if given the opportunity?

URGENT VS. MEANINGFUL

When you are laser focused only on what is right in front of you, you treat every challenge equally. That is what Marie did: both the meeting and the surgery were treated as equally important. Truth be told, we all do that—and therein lies the problem. The options in front of us about how to spend our time *are not equal.* They may feel equal, especially the tasks and opportunities that have become the norm, that others deem important, and that are celebrated and rewarded with tangible and immediate feedback. Today there are even more time demands that fit into this category: unnecessary or unproductive meetings, social media, overinvolvement in extracurricular activities, or anything that feels urgent even though in the grand scheme of life it isn't. There is an art to choosing well when so many demands vie for our attention. So we must learn to choose the meaningful.

#MEANINGFULOVERURGENT

WHAT IS MEANINGFUL?

To be meaningful is to be significant, relevant, important, consequential, or *worthwhile*. Worth your while—worthy of your time.

So to have an appreciation for the meaningful is to first have an appreciation for the value of your own time. If you don't value it, you will be more likely to spend it doing things not worthy of it. You must recognize the preciousness of the gift of time you have been given.

Is it possible that when our insecurities devalue our sense of worth, we spend more of our time on people and things that are not worthy of it? I believe this to be so. It becomes harder to say no to requests that are not meaningful, harder to set boundaries with those who want to use or abuse our time, and easier to waste time proving our worth to those who don't want to see it.

Is it possible that when we take for granted the gift of time, we are more likely to squander that gift and find ourselves living in regret? It's not only possible but probable. When we take for granted the gift of time, we spend it as though our lives are a dress rehearsal and we'll get to come back later for the real performance. But life rarely grants us do-overs. We must choose what is meaningful *now*. Today. In this very moment. We must ask constantly, "What is worthy of my time?" and pursue what is meaningful in a way that is meaningful.

A potent measure of meaning is timelessness. What is meaningful today will also be meaningful tomorrow or next year or even decades from now. The meaningful moments of your life so far were not just meaningful in the moment they occurred. They still hold meaning for you today. They taught you something, moved your life in an important direction, opened a door that otherwise would have remained closed, or made an impact that was significant to someone else. Meaningful is timeless. It transcends the moment.

Spent in meaningful ways, your time can build a life you are excited to live, heal and build relationships, and create a positive legacy that multiplies your impact. But if your perspective is skewed about the true value of your time, you won't see the urgency of making a change.

TIMELESS LIVING

I learned timeless living from my paternal grandparents. The meaningfulness of how they chose to spend their time was aligned with the natural pace of a spiritually grounded life that prioritized relationships and people, and a pace that gave them the margin to invest in what they valued. I spent seven summers with them between the ages of three and eleven, when my grandmother died. My cousins also spent summers there, which made the visits even more fun and memorable. I can't tell you what time I awoke each day during those summers, only that the rooster was my alarm clock. To this day, when I hear a rooster crow, I picture myself opening my eyes and feeling the brightness of the sun shining through the window directly over my head. By the time I woke up, Granddaddy was off to work and Grandmama was likely tending her garden or collecting eggs from her chicken coop.

Every afternoon, starting around three or four o'clock, we all ended up under the big apple tree that separated the backyard from her garden. We sat on the metal foldout chairs beneath the tree, enjoyed the shade, and chatted while we shucked corn or strung green beans for dinner. After a while, Granddaddy would pull up from work in his powder-blue Chevy pickup truck. Oftentimes he'd bring a roadside treat such as watermelon or cantaloupe. I was the only one in the family too finicky to like either, but I loved the excitement and energy of his arrival and listening to everyone rate the tastiness of whatever fruit he'd brought home.

While we certainly enjoyed our share of game shows and Carol Burnett reruns, most of our summer days were spent outside. My cousins and I would play hopscotch and tag, catch lightning bugs and put them in jars with holes poked into the top, and enjoy snacks from the fruit trees around my grandparents' home; peaches, apples, blackberries, plums, and blueberries were always just a few steps away. Sometimes I helped my grandmother hang clothes on the clothesline in her garden as we chatted about random topics. I recall handing her clothespins one morning as she mentioned casually in conversation that she was fifty-nine years old. I had never contemplated that age before, and I tried to wrap my five-year-old head around it. *If I lived to be that old, what would I do with all that time?* I wondered.

Six years later, during our last summer, it seemed perhaps she was aware that her time in this life was nearly up. Granddaddy had died two years earlier, and I imagine the loneliness of losing her husband of nearly forty years had been deeply heartbreaking. She had begun prefacing future plans with the phrase, "If uh live." It frightened me, especially because I had also begun having premonitions that it was our last summer together. And so I willed myself to savor our moments and vividly store the memories in my mind.

One day, as we sat on the front porch snapping peas, she told me about something she was going to do for the church next year "if she lived."

"Grandmama," I said with a tinge of anxiety in my voice. "Why do you keep saying that? I don't like that. It makes me scared."

"Because tomorrow is not promised," she said matter-of-factly. She spoke the truth with a softness that assured me all would be well. "The Bible says do not boast about tomorrow for you do not know what tomorrow will bring," she continued. She told me she wasn't worried and I shouldn't be either. She seemed at peace with the fact that life is not forever. She was also confident that when her time came, she would pass from the finite time of this world to the eternal time of heaven.

Just a few months later, my grandmother passed away. The scene at her funeral gave me a glimpse of what she'd done with her sixty-five years. I was eleven years old and devastated by the loss of two grandparents in two years. Theirs had been my second home. As I sat in the front row with family, I could feel the presence of many people behind me. I turned around out of curiosity to see the faces who'd come to pay their last respects to my beloved grandmother.

The crowd was so large it was standing room only. And the image that has stuck with me all of these years is that of three gas station attendants standing along the wall of the chapel in their navy-blue coveralls with white patches bearing their first names stitched in script. They held their hats in their hands in front of them. These men were not family. They were not even family friends. But they'd heard that Mrs. Burton died, and they took time off from their jobs to honor her.

Even at that young age, I was moved by the idea that your life could touch individuals in such a way that even the people who pump your gas and tune up your car would miss you when you're gone. From the outpouring of condolences from students who'd come through her lunch line to the genuine love of the many children she raised as her own, she had clearly spent her time making choices that were meaningful.

Grandmama didn't fall victim to false urgencies. Instead, she was clear about what mattered. She and Granddaddy kept five grandkids all summer. All these decades later, I have told stories about those summers to hundreds of thousands of people when I am onstage because the lessons they taught were so powerful. I keep her picture on my desk and see her face daily, reminding me to love people, to be humble, and to be brave.

Grandmama understood what we all innately know but too often lose sight of: life is not about how much you can pack into your days but about the impact you can make with your days—especially when that impact touches people. Time is finite, but your legacy is not.

PRESSURED LIVING

Perhaps you had summers similar to mine, or at least summers absent a schedule and structure. But for kids today, summers have changed. Few children know the freedom of roaming outdoors for hours, enjoying technology-free play, or spending abundant time with extended family. Day and overnight camps have replaced free play as more and more families consist of two working parents, a working single parent, or parents wanting to give their children an edge with summer learning opportunities. According to the American Camp Association, summer camps are now an eighteen-billion-dollar industry.[1]

Consider the following comparisons:

UNSTRUCTURED SUMMERS OF DAYS PAST	STRUCTURED SUMMERS OF MODERN TIMES
Awareness of time was based mostly on the natural rhythms of the sun, the heat, and hunger pangs telling you it's time for lunch.	An awareness of time is based on ever-present mobile phones and a regimented schedule.
Kids created their own schedules together outside, including creative games and walking or biking around the neighborhood.	Adults create the schedule for the day, often mostly consisting of indoor and tightly supervised activities.
Kids learned by independent learning and exploration, including navigating conflict and challenges.	Kids learn by directed learning and exploration, and conflicts and challenges often are managed by adults.
Kids came in when the sun went down.	Kids get picked up when parents get off work.
Parents felt safe with their kids playing and exploring beyond their own front porches.	Parents are afraid for their kids to venture beyond their own front porches.

The amount of time kids spend outdoors has dropped drastically in recent decades. Only 10 percent of children spend time outdoors on a daily basis, according to a nationwide survey by the Nature Conservatory.[2] Children today spend more than 90 percent of their free time indoors, and during the summer, much of that time is now spent alone with personalized technology that is rarely enjoyed as a family activity like television was just twenty or thirty years ago. Instead, technology is often an individual indulgence that isolates the watcher from the environment and people around them. That is the new normal.

Increased screen time and structured play have negative consequences on development, according to the American Academy of Pediatrics.[3] But the consequences aren't true for just children. Adults are dealing more and more with the anxiety, sleep disruption, and health challenges that arise from too much screen time and too little relaxation and time in nature.

Much of the new normal of dual-working households and over-scheduled kids and adults seems to be rooted in a collective angst many of us have: the fear that our future is not secure, that our kids' futures are not secure, that we must work more to make more, that our kids need more structured camps and classes and extracurricular activities to give them an advantage in a world that is increasingly competitive.

Generation X is the first generation in American history to be poorer than their parents,[4] and the economic picture appears even dimmer for Millennials.[5] For those born in the mid-1980s, just 50 percent earn more than their parents did.[6] Not long ago, the American dream could be secured with the foundation of a high school education and a job that did not require a college degree. Today, only 36 percent of jobs require only a high school diploma, according to the Bureau of Labor Statistics,[7] and those jobs typically do not pay enough to live a middle-class lifestyle.

Getting into the top colleges is harder than it has ever been. For example, for the class of 2001, which was accepted to college in 1997, the admission rate at Stanford University was 15.5 percent and the admission rate at Harvard was 12.3 percent. For the class of 2021, accepted in 2017, the admission rate was 5.2 percent at Stanford and 4.7 percent at Harvard.[8] These schools, whose acceptance rates twenty years ago were their lowest in history at the time, now have twice as many applicants and an admission rate three times more selective. No wonder so many parents are trying to get their kids involved in as many activities as possible to help them stand out from the crowd. And once they get into that great college, these kids continue overscheduling themselves so they can land that great career. The new normal for them is just normal. They've lived it their entire lives.

My grandparents' world, even my parents' world, was one in which the aspiration of living the American dream was much lower. The pressure to work more and earn more, to stand out from the crowd and take on debt, was simply not as immense. And the constant pull of distractions, brought on by technology, was minimal. So while the definition of what is meaningful has not changed, the ability to make meaningful choices has become more difficult.

WHAT IS "URGENT"?

Just as there are timeless choices, there are also false urgencies. We call these activities "urgent," but they will mean little or nothing in the future. You may not even remember why they were important or who they involved. These are the things we treat as urgent, but they are *false* urgencies—like the meeting Marie attended the morning her father died. It is imperative to learn the difference.

We are intentionally bombarded with messages that wear away at the boundary between real and created urgency. I'm guessing that, like me, you've had the experience of getting breaking news alerts across your television screen or cell phone, and within seconds you realize the news is not actually anything breaking at all. In the 1980s, breaking news really was breaking news. It was the urgent news that everyone needed to know—now! Breaking news was a public service of sorts that meant a major and sudden military action was taking place or a tornado was about to rip through your town. Then, starting sometime in the 1990s, as networks were forced to fight harder to keep the attention of viewers, breaking news instead became a way to get us to stop changing the channel and watch. As we will discuss later in this book, so many of today's distractions and temptations are rooted in commercial motives.

What are some of the most common false urgencies?

- When we pick up the phone in the middle of dinner because we heard the text message chime or we want to check our social media feeds
- When we choose to multitask rather than give our full attention to the people right in front of us
- When we give up on the idea that a full night's sleep is a reasonable expectation because we just don't have time
- When we struggle to see the big picture and constantly make decisions by focusing only on what's happening today, without thinking about the consequences that could come tomorrow

False urgency steals time from the things that are meaningful. Your to-do list may feel urgent. Your self-imposed deadlines may stress you out. But what if you stepped back and asked yourself, "What is the most *meaningful* choice I can make right now?"

LIVING IN TIME POVERTY

Nearly three years ago I stumbled on an article that led to the series of events that has me writing this book. I was probably procrastinating (that's what I'm usually doing when I read random articles while surfing the internet), but I don't remember for sure. What I do know is that the content of a *New York Times* opinion piece called "No Money, No Time" got my full attention.[9] I stopped what I was doing. I leaned forward as I read, devouring the information as though the knowledge might actually change my life.

Just what was so intriguing to me about the article? It introduced me to a phrase I'd never heard before: *time poverty*. The article's author, Maria Konnikova, described the "time debt" she creates when she needs an extension on deadlines to complete an assignment:

> My experience is the time equivalent of a high-interest loan cycle, except instead of money, I borrow time. But this kind of borrowing comes with an interest rate of its own: By focusing on one immediate deadline, I neglect not only future deadlines but the mundane tasks of daily life that would normally take up next to no time or mental energy.[10]

I've mentioned the term *time poverty*, but let me define it fully here. According to Harvard economist Sendhil Mullainathan, two new types of poverty have emerged in society: time poverty and bandwidth poverty.[11] Time poverty occurs when we accumulate time debt from too many obligations that require our time. It is being in persistent time debt and continually borrowing from the future, falling behind, and feeling the pressure of never being able to catch up. Bandwidth poverty is a shortage of attention due to the constant use of our cognitive resources. In other words, when we have too much to do, our mental energy gets stretched thin and we have an attention shortage, so much so that it can impact the decisions we make, our stress levels, and our commitments.

So we are in time debt when we keep saying yes to new things even when we don't have time to finish what's already in front of us. But the bandwidth problem comes when we are just doing way too much at the same time—keeping up with our kids' schedules and our own, too many projects, school requests, fitness goals, volunteer work, bills, car repairs, family needs, and the list goes on.

According to the article, I was time poor. I had never articulated it quite that way before.

The content spoke to me so deeply and the implications of it so bothered me that I printed out the article and laid it in plain view on a shelf in my closet, to make sure I would not forget I had a problem that needed solving. Every morning when I went into my closet, I was reminded that I didn't want to be time poor. I also didn't know how to stop being time poor. *But I wanted to.* If I could just keep reminding myself of that fact, then maybe, just maybe, I could dig my way out of the hole I was in.

I soon printed another copy for safekeeping in my laptop bag. Occasionally, on a trip I'd pull it out and stare at it, unsure of what to do with the knowledge it contained but certain I needed to make the change the article spoke of.

Why did this article so deeply resonate with me that I carried it around with me for the better part of a year, hoping that somehow through osmosis I might make some changes? In my twenties, my biggest stressor was the financial debt I had accumulated—not because I was ill or faced unexpected tragedy, but because I was an impatient and emotional spender. One night while I was praying for the miracle of a heap of money to pay off my credit cards, car loan, and student loans, I had a sudden revelation that the path to financial freedom would come only by changing my attitude about debt. It took me three years of staying out of clothing stores, learning to negotiate higher pay, and getting clear that no amount of stuff and no brand name could ever bring the satisfaction that comes from not owing anyone anything.

So when the idea of debt was presented as it relates to time, it really hit me. After working so hard to climb out of financial debt years ago, the realization that I'd piled up a different type of debt—time debt— felt deflating. It also felt like a challenge, an opportunity to climb out and find new freedom. The process of digging out of time debt does indeed parallel the process of climbing out of financial debt. I believe avoiding time debt is far more vital to our well-being, though. While money is a renewable resource, time is not.

CHOOSING TO SHIFT FROM "NORMAL" TO NATURAL

Looking back, Marie still asks herself, "What daughter would forgo seeing her dad before surgery for a meeting?" She asks the question rhetorically, the implication being that the kind of daughter who makes the decision she made is not a good one. But I believe there is a more compassionate and accurate explanation. The kind of daughter who makes the decision she made is a daughter living in time poverty. She is someone with no margin. Hers is a soul so pressed for time that she loses her perspective, because in order to function daily, she must be narrowly focused on what's right in front of her—carrying out as many tasks as possible as quickly as possible. This way of being has become her normal, and she rarely veers from it because to do so could create a domino effect of problems. But it is possible to climb out of time poverty. It is possible to make new choices.

But first, we have to gain perspective. The problem of time feels more pressing today because it is harder to gain control over our time. Over the next few chapters, we will delve into the reasons why. This is an important step I don't want you to miss, because we are at a unique point in history. The world we live in today is more demanding than the world our parents and grandparents and even we grew up in. There are more options and distractions. Your brain isn't wired for what you deal with daily, and if you're not careful, the way you react to the environment you have been thrust into can literally make you feel as though it's nearly impossible to change.

. . . .

MEANINGFUL MINUTE

Take a quick minute to answer this question:

What's at stake for you if you continue on the path of trying to do too much in too little time? What meaningful moments and opportunities might you miss?

_____

_____

_____

_____

CHAPTER TWO

IS IT EVER ENOUGH?

Six thirty a.m. The alarm clock blared from Julie's smartphone, and she rolled over to hit snooze. As on most mornings, she didn't go back to sleep but used the nine-minute delay to linger under the cozy softness of her down comforter.

Impulsively, she reached over to pick up the phone from her nightstand and tapped the mail app. She had read articles explaining you should never check email first thing in the morning, but this had become her habit. *Maybe I can clear out a few messages before I get out of bed*, she thought optimistically. There were seven new messages since she turned out the lights around 10:15 p.m.—one of them marked urgent from her boss. The rest were replies to his email about an upset customer, which he sent at 10:38 p.m. and on which he copied her and two other colleagues. As she read the message traffic, she saw that both of her colleagues had already replied with possible solutions and committed to getting to the office early to help fix the problem.

Good grief. Do these people never stop working? The one night I finally get to sleep at a decent hour and everyone at my office is on email!

Heightened expectations, brought on by new norms of technology that make us accessible twenty-four hours a day, create a special kind of pressure when everyone around you jumps on the bandwagon. When the expectation is that you are always available, and others around you rise to that expectation, choosing not to be available can come with unwanted consequences. Will you be labeled the slacker? The one too busy with other priorities to be fully committed? Even if you are more productive than everyone else during regular work hours, will being unresponsive to after-hours communication give the appearance of you not being "all in"? Increased expectations make the stakes of competitiveness higher than ever.

Technology has made life easier in so many ways—and more complicated in others. As saved time gets eaten up by new activities, where exactly does that time go? Often it simply goes toward the quest to do more. So saved time simply puts us on a treadmill of efficiency. If the new normal is doing too much with too little time, technology is the engine that makes the new normal operate. That little piece of technology we so inaccurately refer to as our "phone" is a computer we carry around everywhere we go and keep within arm's reach. Tasks we used to focus on only at a desk are now possible to carry out before we even get out of bed. The boundaries are blurred, and everyone expects them to be. You can get more done, and you can get it done at any hour, from any location.

What are some of the heightened expectations?

- Being available anytime, anywhere
- Having access to others anytime, anywhere
- Having it all—career, family, looks, financial success
- Spending time managing your image on social media
- Investing time earning a four-year degree or in specialized training as a minimum qualification for a middle-class career

These heightened expectations generally fall into three categories: our expectations of ourselves, others' expectations of us, and our expectations of others.

OUR EXPECTATIONS OF OURSELVES

We expect things of ourselves, our lives, and our abilities that previous generations simply did not—and in many ways, could not. Those born in the 1970s and later, especially women, know the pressure of trying to have it all. We were told we could and should have a great career, an impressive income, a successful husband, well-behaved children, the perfect home, and a fit body. And try to pull it all off by age thirty, ideally. The expectations for women in recent decades have been higher than for any women in history.

So many of women's anxieties center around life not looking the way we had planned. In other words, expectations not being met. If you compare your circumstances to those of the people you believe are effortlessly juggling having it all, it's easy to wonder why *you* don't have it all figured out.

Social media and an abundance of reality television shows expose us to the lives of people we don't know, creating a natural tendency to compare our lives to unrealistic standards. While scripted shows certainly impact us, the premise is that they are fictional. But shows that supposedly celebrate the lives of regular people suggest unrealistic standards are perfectly normal. *Upward social comparison* is the psychological term for the tendency to compare ourselves with those we perceive as doing better than we are. If we compare only upward, our perception of what normal looks like becomes unrealistic.

In today's world, do we want more and expect more superficial things than past generations did? If so, how does that impact how we choose to spend our time? And if indeed the norms of what we want and expect have changed, then how do we undo the thinking that leads to automatically committing more time to earning money in order to have more of what we want?

With advertising custom-tailored to our likes based on our social media profiles, geographic locations, and demographics, we are constantly bombarded with the message of "more." And that cannot help but influence our expectations. Resisting a constant message about what we don't have but ought to have, and even deserve, takes sheer willpower. Ever felt perfectly fine with where you live until you turn on HGTV and watch a couple house hunting for their second home with a million-dollar budget or renovating their entire house with the help of an amazing designer? It is immensely entertaining, but when it's over, it is easy to start looking around your own house and feeling discontent because it doesn't measure up.

The amount of time we spend on social media has changed the way many of us see our lives—on constant display for everyone to like, react to, and comment about. In 2017, Facebook, Instagram, and YouTube users spent an average of fifty minutes per day on those sites.[1] Prior to the early 2000s, most people lived privately with no internet imprint to speak of unless they were a celebrity, politician, or entrepreneur with a website. Then along came MySpace. Remember that? Next, Facebook decided to expand beyond college students to become a site for everybody. Suddenly, we could all have an online presence— for free, and for no other reason than to connect. But early on, few of us thought about how time-consuming social media could become or how it can create upward social comparisons that drain our joy. Fear of missing out (FOMO) is real, and it can drive us to add activities and expectations to our lives that we don't have time for. It is a prime example of false urgency.

The truth is, it's okay to miss out. In certain seasons of life and work, we must make peace with missing out because it is simply impossible to do everything. In fact, with the right perspective we can even find joy in missing out when we see our choices as a sign of personal growth. We must put our stake in the ground and decide what really matters, even though it's harder to do when the opportunities for comparison are so abundant. What expectations do you have of yourself that drain your time and create unnecessary pressure?

OTHERS' EXPECTATIONS OF US

It isn't always our expectations that create the most pressure. If we're honest, we'll admit we sometimes change our behavior to meet the expectations others might have of us. At work, expectations have risen a lot. In many industries, more productivity and more accessibility have become the norm. Most people are motivated to rise to the level of expectation because there is a reward—acceptance, job security, admiration, money.

During the recession that hit in 2008, many companies downsized. Many people ended up taking on the responsibilities of their laid-off coworkers. So one person might have a job that was previously done by two or three people. Expectations for performance rose for those who held on to their jobs. Motivated to remain employed, they made adjustments to get the work done, even though it required more time, focus, and energy. Then, seeing that more was being accomplished with fewer workers, companies were not motivated to hire to their same levels of previous staffing. Why would they? The work was getting done with fewer people.

It is a shift that is easier to deal with if you have time and energy to spare. But what if you are raising children? Or taking care of a parent? Or both? Higher expectations at work can mean less time and energy for your family, but the family responsibilities remain. To meet the demands of both, you may find yourself working during personal time—checking emails while you're cooking, taking work calls on the way to your child's soccer practice, or bringing your laptop on vacation. Those who are parents and caretakers can feel penalized if they can't stay late or be as available after hours because they may be passed over for opportunities as a result. But those who don't have families may feel unfairly burdened with a greater workload and an expectation to do more because they don't have family responsibilities.

Heightened expectations in the workplace mean we must make

intentional choices in the midst of what can feel like never-ending demands at work and home. Using the measure of meaningful over urgent is an important start. Rather than becoming distracted by the small-picture issues, we must keep our eyes on what's meaningful for the company over the false urgencies.

It is not just work expectations that have been heightened. It is personal expectations too. If you were around in the not-so-distant past, you remember having to time your phone calls for when someone would be home—and you didn't call during dinner. The phone was shared by everyone in the house, so if someone else was on the phone, they'd take a message and pass it along, and then you'd wait for a call back. Now that everyone has a personal phone, or rather *a multifunctional computer*, on them at all times, the expectation is that we are always reachable. Forget leaving a voice mail; if we don't answer, they'll text us and expect a response right away.

Today our kids can reach us anytime as well. For most, calling your parents at work in the '80s and '90s was a big deal. You might even have to explain why you were calling and convince a boss or secretary that your parent needed to stop work to come talk to you. Now we can be reached by our children all day long, which has its advantages, but being able to stay focused isn't one of them.

OUR EXPECTATIONS OF OTHERS

The last type of expectation is really a symptom of having too much on your plate. No one likes to admit it, but do you ever find yourself irritated with the slow cashier at the grocery store—the one who wants to have a conversation with every customer who comes through her line—when you are in a hurry? Have you ever yelled in your car at the person in front of you because he didn't take off as soon as the light turned green? Have you been impatient with someone because you felt inconvenienced, frustrated, or pressed for time? With less time available to do what we need to do, we have less tolerance for those who take up our time. The temptation is to be less generous with our time yet expect others to be generous with theirs.

We live in an era when we really don't have to wait for anything. We expect access to what and who we want no matter where we are or when we are there—Wi-Fi in coffee shops, airplanes, and retail stores; twenty-four-hour customer service; and phone apps that allow you to transfer money, deposit checks, and speak face-to-face with someone halfway around the world are just a few examples. We expect same-day delivery, can summon a car to pick us up in under two minutes with the click of an app, and the term *google* is now a verb that indicates we can have an answer to anything within seconds. We expect our needs to be met instantly, and that means we can become demanding and impatient if we are not careful. We can assign urgency to things that don't require it and lack patience for the things that are meaningful.

THE PROBLEM WITH HEIGHTENED EXPECTATIONS

Heightened expectations set the bar higher for what life needs to look like in order for us to feel successful and content, but lower expectations actually increase happiness. Surveys of nearly every country in the world have consistently shown that one of the happiest countries is Denmark.[2] The Danish are happier than even their Scandinavian counterparts in Sweden and Norway. Researchers were perplexed by this fact until they dug a little deeper into findings. That's when they discovered the Danes have lower expectations for what their lives should look like. To be clear, it isn't that they have low expectations, just lower expectations than folks in neighboring countries. When asked at the start of a year what their hopes are for the coming year, the bar is markedly lower. With expectations a little lower, happiness is easier to attain and maintain. There is less pressure all around.

Think about that for a moment: What would it look like if you adjusted your expectations?

To choose what is meaningful is to clarify for yourself which expectations you are willing to meet and which ones you are not.

Our souls crave meaning. The gratification of a checked-off to-do list can feel like a triumph, and some days it truly is. But at some point, we have to know that what we choose to spend our time doing daily has significance beyond simply getting things done. Deep down, we want to know that the goals we invest our time pursuing will yield more than the praise and admiration of those who are impressed by superficial signs of success. Praise is a tempting substitute for meaning. After all, if everybody thinks you are successful, aren't you?

The problem that occurs too often is that we equate busyness with significance. Busyness has become a status symbol. We see someone stretched for time as someone who is in demand. And if you are in demand, you must be important. Meaning is defined as significance, importance, relevance, and that which is worthwhile. But when we mistake busyness for importance, we pursue it in our search for meaning, and we devalue rest, leisure, and play, all of which are essential to healthy functioning.

BUSYNESS IS THE NEW LEISURE

"What is the week . . . *end*?"

This famous line from the former PBS show *Downton Abbey* was uttered by the aristocratic Violet Crawley, the fictional Countess of Grantham, as she processed the meaning of a word new to her vocabulary: *weekend*. For a titled, wealthy, seventy-something woman of leisure in early 1900s Great Britain, the idea of five days of work followed by a highly anticipated, two-day personal break was entirely foreign. Just close your eyes and imagine it for a moment—a schedule in which all days are equal. You can do whatever you want, or don't want, to do. Weeks and weekends blend together without the constraint of work schedules and days off. There are no Mondays to dread, no humps to get over, and no weekends to live for.

Sounds dreamy, doesn't it? *Where does one sign up to be a countess?*

For centuries, leisure time has been a status symbol. It signals to the world a life free from the encumbrance of work because you have enough money to live without the need for a steady paycheck. You can focus your time on whatever interests you with no pressure to be in any particular place at any particular time. It is the ultimate symbol of wealth. In Western Europe, leisure time is still a status symbol. People are working less, not more, in Europe than they were a few decades ago. Some European companies have even implemented "no email after work" policies in addition to the standard six weeks or more of vacation. But in the United States, the status symbol has shifted from leisure to busyness.[3] Just a couple of decades ago, the perks of being in management included long, leisurely lunches and Fridays on the golf course. But today, a higher income means more work hours. Leisure time in the United States is more a symbol of low status than high. And you can tell by how we talk.

Listen in on conversations and notice how often, "How are you?" is answered with, "I'm soooo busy." It is a humblebrag with the hidden message, "I'm important. I'm needed. I'm in demand." Being in demand at work can imply financial success and upward mobility. Being busy at home signals a full home life and conveys that your family has it together—and the reason is because of you. But if we dig a bit deeper, there's more at work than simply the humblebrag. Busyness is now a status symbol in America, and it's also a dangerous threat to our well-being that sets up the expectation of overwork and overload as a norm.

America is a country that has always valued hard work. We celebrate the person who "pulls himself up by his bootstraps," the self-made millionaire, and "rags to riches" stories of success. This line of thinking is ingrained in the idea of the American dream. But what exactly is this American dream that we so frequently speak of and long for?

Coined by the writer James Truslow Adams in his 1931 book *The Epic of America*, the phrase "the American dream" refers to "that dream of a land in which life should be better and richer and fuller for everyone, with opportunity for each according to ability or achievement."[4] Having a richer and fuller life became synonymous with having more money and more possessions, and in order to acquire more, people generally had to work longer and harder. Staying overworked and overly busy became a conduit through which the American dream was seemingly achieved. But even in the '30s, Adams could see that Americans were off track, misinterpreting the dream and pursuing the wrong things: "It is not a dream of motor cars and high wages merely, but a dream of a social order in which each man and each woman shall be able to attain to the fullest stature of which they are innately capable, and be recognized by others for what they are, regardless of the fortuitous circumstances of birth or position."[5]

Our skewed priorities in relation to the dream have always been present, and thus countless people have come into this country determined to "work their fingers to the bone" (a phrase we seem to be proud of) to achieve the trappings falsely associated with the dream. We admire the tenacity of someone who "burns the candle at both ends." In our mind, the person who stays busy is the person who will be most rewarded.

Remember Julie, who checked her email after hitting the snooze button only to discover a barrage of emails from her boss and colleagues had flooded her inbox overnight? The stress of feeling compelled to do what everyone else was doing created a lot of anxiety. It was common for her to wake up to emails that had been sent and requests that had been made late in the evening or early in the morning. She didn't initiate a conversation with her boss about it right away. She decided to commit herself even more to being as productive and impactful as possible during regular work hours. She had a chat with her boss about some of the most meaningful goals of her department and her company, then set out to positively and directly impact the achievement of those goals.

Then, after a couple of small wins, she had a heart-to-heart about expectations around email. To her surprise, her boss didn't actually have an expectation that she check and respond to messages late at night. It happened to be a productive time for him to catch up on work, he explained, and he did not expect her to respond until she got to work in the morning. Then he complimented her: "Besides, I know I can count on you to be efficient and get things done when you get in. That's the least of my worries." By facing her fears and looking for a feasible way to choose the meaningful over the urgent, she adjusted work expectations that had caused her stress for too long.

THE GOOD NEWS: YOU CAN ADJUST YOUR EXPECTATIONS

The good news is this: just because expectations and norms have changed doesn't mean we have to adopt them as our own. In fact, we can—and must—do just the opposite. How would your stress level and happiness change if you adjusted your expectations about when you have done "enough"?

I love when serendipity confirms you are on the right path. While I was writing this book and considering how to illustrate the concept of creating your own new normal, my colleague Stella Grizont, a fellow positive psychology coach, shared an experience with me that vividly illustrates the opportunity that lies before each of us when it comes to time and happiness.

On a weekend trip to Arizona with her two best friends, she ended up on a hike—at least that's what *they* called it. Turns out, Stella says, it was more of a climb than a hike. As they approached the popular Camelback Mountain, she remembers thinking it didn't look quite like what she was expecting. Back home in California, her idea of a hike was typically an intense walk on dirt ground with maybe a slight incline, but no rocks or gravel and certainly nothing vertical. Nonetheless, she was up for it.

At first, the hike went quickly as she was lost in deep conversation with her friends. They were midway through before she became quietly alarmed by the intensity of the climb. She started to genuinely feel afraid.

"My foot slipped," she recalls. "The incline started to get steep. Then we reached a bend that was trickier to climb. I thought to myself, *If this is tricky to get up, I cannot imagine how I'm going to get down!*"

Just as her thoughts began to spiral, they took a water break. As the hot desert sun beat down on her legs, she thought about her choice of clothing. Rather than long pants to protect her knees from getting scraped, she'd worn shorts. Instead of her best athletic shoes, she was wearing her casual sneakers. She took a gulp of water and looked around in amazement at the pace of the other hikers.

"There were people prancing around the mountain like little goats," she recalls with a tinge of awe in her voice. "They were just skipping down. Hopping! I was like, *What are they doing?* I actually admired them, and I also felt really aware of my own skill level."

As she sat on a rock with her water bottle, she pondered her fear. She's not normally one to back down from fear, but this was physical fear—and she didn't want to ignore it. It would take about twenty more minutes to get to the top of the mountain, and she didn't know if she could make it—at least not without slipping or twisting an ankle. And then how would she get back down the mountain?

Deep down, though, there was a more basic question: *Do I really want to keep going?*

There is something about moments of fear and frustration that make you begin to question things you don't normally question. Stella closed her eyes for a few seconds and took a breath. *The intention is that you go to the top*, she acknowledged to herself. *But* why *do I need to go to the top? It is beautiful right here. I've challenged myself. I don't see the last 20 percent giving me any more benefit, and it feels dangerous.* She finally decided the reward she'd gain for the additional work she'd have to put forth simply would not be worth it.

"Why would I do it? Just because I would reach the top?" she reflects today. "I didn't care. I checked in with myself and realized: 'I don't really care.'"

So Stella's answer to the question "Do I really want to go to the top?" was a decisive no. It was her moment of choice—a conscious decision she made about whether to lean in to the goal or drop it.

"It just really didn't mean that much to me. I didn't need to prove anything, so I decided to let my friends go on and I would wait for them." But her friends didn't want to leave her sitting in the sun waiting for them. They insisted on turning around and hiking back down the mountain together and didn't make a big deal about it.

As Stella shared this story with me and two other friends, she'd initially labeled the experience a failure. But as she talked through it, she realized it wasn't a failure at all. It was actually a triumph. Abandoning a tough goal that had little meaning for her turned out to be an empowering decision. Rather than succumb to the pressure of the crowd, she'd listened to the truth of her heart's desires. She saved her energy, possibly averted physical danger, and found happiness in taking a hike with her friends without caving to the pressure of expectations that were never her own.

AWAKEN TO YOUR OWN
MOMENT OF CHOICE

Imagine yourself for a moment on that metaphorical mountain. You're well into your hike, gazing up at what you've been told is the pinnacle you ought to reach. It looks lovely, but it doesn't make your heart sing. The pinnacle could be a job you want but hours you don't. It could be a bigger business, but you dread the idea of managing more people. It could be a social or community position that would elevate your status but wear out your soul. It could be the idea of having it all, but you feel the gnawing sensation that you'll be buried under the weight of having it all at the same time.

Now close your eyes and take a breath. Then another. Relax. Then ask yourself this:

In this season of your life, what is the meaningful pinnacle you want to reach?

_____

_____

Deep down, what would feel fulfilling and natural for you?

_____

_____

Stella's experience on the mountain is a metaphor for the life-changing opportunity we all face. When we can see the fear and frustration of being overwhelmed as an opportunity to awaken to our own moment of choice, our journey to authentic happiness begins.

Let's take a deeper look at the metaphor of Stella on Camelback Mountain and how it applies to time and happiness.

- She began her journey not knowing she was embarking on a hike of greater intensity than she was used to. She powered ahead anyway.

  Most of us take on careers, opportunities, and family and community obligations without accurately counting the cost. We are often well into the journey before we realize just how much time, energy, money, and joy it will require.
- She was physically unprepared for the hike.

  Most of us dive into additional commitments before creating our margins—space that gives us the breathing room and resources to get to the destination successfully.
- She recognized and honored her limitations.

  When you feel stressed, you can either ignore your feelings and power through—again and again until you are burned out, neglecting relationships and other commitments—or you can pause and reflect on the next best step forward.
- When she took a break, she had time to reflect. It was then that she realized the goal of getting to the top was not meaningful to her and therefore not worthy of the energy, effort, and risk.

  At critical moments, it is essential to give yourself a break, find a quiet moment, and ask a PQ (powerful question) about what you are doing and why. Even more important, answer with honesty and courage, even if your answers may make you uncomfortable or unpopular if you follow through on the truth. I call this process reflective problem solving—*and it is an essential skill if you want to reverse the new normal of stress that is so prevalent.*

- She clarified that her goals for the hike were met and made a conscious choice to abandon what was the norm for most people on the mountain in favor of what felt natural and fulfilling for her.

  It takes courage to go against the grain, but it is worth it. Be honest with yourself and others about your needs, and you will be liberated to live a life that is authentic to you—the life you were created to live.

- She shifted her interpretation of the experience from one of failure to one of empowerment.

  Refuse to compare your unique version of normal to someone else's. If you do compare, you may find yourself mislabeling something a failure. Instead, embrace the idea that success occurs when you fulfill your divine assignments, not others'.

Heightened expectations about what success and happiness look like can lead you on a path that holds little meaning, at a pace that's dangerous, for a reward that will prove empty. When you get the sense that it's all just too much, you can make an intentional choice—a shift in your expectations about when you've done enough and your definition of success. Making such a shift will go against norms, but it will also refresh your soul. It will quench your thirst for meaning and joy in your everyday life. It will restore a sense of control and purpose. And it may prove challenging. But it's worth it.

WHAT WORKS FOR "EVERYONE" MAY NOT WORK FOR YOU— AND THAT'S OKAY

Certainly climbing to the top of Camelback Mountain holds authentic meaning for some, but not for everyone. And therein lies the problem. Many of the choices we make today reflect a norm that is clearly not natural or meaningful for everyone:

- Feeling constantly pressed for time, running late, or feeling guilty for not being able to get together with friends or family members
- Cramming your week with so many activities and meetings that you have no time to think, plan, or be creative
- Being accessible 24-7, even on vacation, after hours, or when you're not feeling well
- Financing your lifestyle with debt that you have no clear path to pay off in the near future
- Feeling beholden to a job you don't love just to pay the bills

We all have expectations of what our lives will be like, but what we imagine will be a light hike often turns out to be more of an unexpected climb that leaves you fearful and anxious. As you attempt to live up to expectations—both self-imposed and cultural—you begin to realize that the price for meeting those expectations can be very steep. But hey, everyone seems to be climbing that mountain. *It's just life. It's what you have to do.*

Looking around, it can appear that everyone else has it all figured out. Trying to keep up with the pace and expectations can feel exhausting and bewildering. "How do they do it? Are they not exhausted too?" But if you keep climbing long enough, you come to a point at which you start questioning the purpose of the journey. "Why am I doing this?" "What does it mean to me?" "What do I really need?" When you get to that point—and maybe you're arriving there now—it is a moment of choice, an awakening of sorts. It's your opportunity to decide what your expectations are for your life, to choose those expectations rather than allowing them to choose you.

MEANINGFUL MINUTE

What expectation do you embrace, not because it is meaningful to you, but because it is the norm everyone else embraces? How much time could you reclaim if you adjusted or rejected that expectation?

_____

_____

_____

_____

CHAPTER THREE

TIME POOR, TECH BLOATED

In 1930, the world's foremost economist at the time, John Maynard Keynes, proclaimed with confidence that his generation's grandchildren would work about three hours a day and only if they wanted to.[1] Technology of the time—from household appliances to cars to industrial advances—had saved so much time and made life so much easier that experts wondered what future generations would do with so much free time.

As one of the grandchildren of Keynes's generation, I think it's safe to say his prediction sounds pretty laughable to us now. But at the time, it was quite sensible and, frankly, exciting.

In Keynes's world, it was assumed that the purpose of technological progress was to make life easier and more leisurely. But ask the average American and she'll likely explain that her life is more demanding than her parents' ever was. The expectations are higher, and the 24-7 accessibility is exhausting. The reality of so many of our lives is a far cry from the way Keynes and others predicted twenty-first-century life would be.

If we'd lived in the world Keynes inhabited in 1930, I bet we'd have agreed with him. I can just picture myself daydreaming with delight about how leisurely life would be—and how much happier I would become. Each time a new technology emerged, I might have boasted even more about this workless future we all would soon enjoy. Without precedent for so many advances or knowledge of the coming events and technology, the assumption was that advances were ultimately meant to benefit people.

Positive-psychology researchers have warned for years now about the "hedonic treadmill," the idea that we are poor predictors of what will make us happy. On a hedonic treadmill, we adapt to continually improving circumstances. So the new car you believed would make you happy gives you a boost of joy for a little while, and then you get used to it as it becomes your new normal. Soon you are daydreaming about the next new thing that could make you happier. You take steps that *feel* like you're moving forward, but you're not actually going anywhere. You are on a treadmill.

It seems we are also poor predictors of the impact of changing norms, so much so that we are in danger of becoming the proverbial frog in boiling water who doesn't notice the cool water has become hot because it happened so gradually. He could jump out at any time, but he doesn't even try until it is too late. Over the last fifty years, as technology and cultural changes have afforded us more choices and faster options, we have essentially stepped onto an *efficiency treadmill*. As we "save" time, we simply increase expectations. The hectic pace, addictive technology, and overflowing schedules that define so many of our lives have happened little by little. As we get used to more, it becomes our new normal.

Think about it. Not so long ago, one-hour photo shops could be found every few blocks. You could drop off your camera film and get pics back the same afternoon. Your eyes might have been closed in half the pictures, but you didn't know until you got them back. At the turn of this century, none of us had a Facebook or LinkedIn profile, no Instagram or Twitter or Snapchat. No consumer had ever heard the terms *YouTube* or *iPhone*. The idea of video-calling someone through your cell phone would have conjured up images of the space-age cartoon *The Jetsons*. Text messages were entirely too cumbersome to send because each letter corresponded with a number on your flip phone. Music was still something you went to the store to buy on CDs. And when you wanted to get online at home, you used your dial-up internet connection through your telephone, likely greeted with a lovely voice proclaiming, "You've got mail!"

Since 2000, time and how we spend it have accelerated at warp speed. Cell phone use is universal. Text messaging became so popular that we now use our phones to text more than we use them to make phone calls.[2] Social media became the norm, giving all of us a platform to put our thoughts and lives on display and get a glimpse into everyone else's. Then the smartphone was born, putting it all at your fingertips with a personal mini-computer that gives you access to everything, everywhere, all the time.

To be clear, the connectivity that twenty-first-century technology gives us has its upsides. The world feels smaller because communication is faster and easier. And while it can at times feel like we are connected to too many people, those connections can open doors and opportunities we might not otherwise experience.

I connected with my own husband, a middle- and high-school classmate of mine while growing up in Colorado, because we were Facebook friends. He saw my book *Successful Women Think Differently* in an airport bookstore and jokingly tagged me in a post that said, "Should I get this book?" Through back-and-forth online banter, we realized we lived in the same city 1,500 miles from where we grew up. We had simultaneously lived in three cities (Denver, Dallas, and

Atlanta) for a total of seventeen years of our lives, but it was social media that ultimately connected us. Two decades after graduating high school, we had lunch. The rest is history. We owe Facebook founder Mark Zuckerberg a long-overdue thank-you note. Technology can be a conduit for positive connection, but it can also be an ever-present distraction and time drain.

NO STOPPING CUES

Remember what it was like to read the newspaper? Or time dinner and finishing the dishes so that you'd be ready to sit down and watch your favorite show when it came on at exactly eight o'clock? No? It might feel like a lifetime ago, but not so long ago media was consumed at specific times and in specific amounts. You watched one episode of your favorite show at a time. Binge watching on your favorite app was not an option. Reading the news meant reading the stories the paper contained *that day*. But go to any news site or app today and you will encounter a bottomless pit of stories. You get to the end of one and there is a suggestion for three more to read. In fact, there are probably links in the story you are reading to other related stories the media outlet wants you to read. Psychologist Adam Alter, author of *Irresistible: The Rise of Addictive Technology and the Business of Keeping Us Hooked,* points out a major addictive quality to modern media— there is no natural stopping point.[3] This lack of "stopping cues," as Alter calls them, means there is always another article or news post to read, another episode to watch. Have you ever scrolled to the very bottom of a social media feed? Try it. There *is* no bottom. If there was, you might actually shut the app down and move on to something else.

Awareness of this simple but profound point can help you see why it is important to intentionally choose meaningful habits that introduce stopping cues that shift your attention. For example, set your phone to limit addictive apps to a certain amount of time each day. Once you meet your limit, you must enter a password to continue. This makes you stop and think. Or choose a simple rule, such as watching one episode per week of your favorite show or putting your phone in another room at meal times.

TECHNOLOGY SAVES TIME— AND CONSUMES TIME

Keynes was right. Advances over the last several decades have certainly saved time. Most technological innovation has been about saving time and making us more efficient. From traveling to cooking and cleaning to delivering information, the time savings is astonishing. Just imagine for a moment carrying your twenty-first-century technology into the 1930s world. Take laundry, for example. The multiday task of washing clothes in the 1930s involved soaking them overnight, heating water and filling washtubs, scrubbing the clothes on a washboard, rinsing them, and then rolling them through a hand-operated mangle to squeeze out the excess water. Then you'd hang them on a clothesline outside or on a clotheshorse next to the fireplace or kitchen. And finally, after all the steam of wash day had cleared out of your house, you'd get out your irons, heat them (electric irons were still a luxury), and iron each piece of clothing.

I'm sorry. What?

Just imagine having a modern-day washer and dryer plopped into your 1930s life. Suddenly a task that may have taken two full days of intense labor takes just a few hours of intermittent attention. Suddenly you've "saved" a ton of time. You can kick up your feet, rest, play a game, or do whatever you want.

As I said earlier, we adapt to continually improving circumstances, and therefore advances in technology don't convert to less work or more leisure. Instead, they tend to lead to one of two things: (1) taking on more and more in less and less time or (2) finding new ways to fill our saved time.

The end result is this: we don't have more free time. Instead, we are time poor. Many of us live in a state of time poverty where we constantly feel deprived of enough time to do everything we want to get done, spend quality moments with the people we care about, and rest.

Since 1965, women with children have dramatically increased their time driving and watching television, and significantly decreased time spent playing with their children, doing chores, and exercising. In 1965, mothers with children ages five to eighteen spent fourteen more hours per week being physically active rather than sedentary, according to a 2013 report in *Mayo Clinic Proceedings*.[4] By 2010, moms in this same category spent nearly four more hours being sedentary rather than physically active. Sedentary activity includes non-work-related time spent driving as well as using mobile devices, televisions, and computers. Certainly none of us wants to go back to a time when physical activity included scrubbing clothes on a washboard, physically wringing them through a mangle, and hanging them up to dry, but being glued to mobile devices and being stuck in traffic are not exactly ideal alternatives.

It is essential that we begin intentionally choosing how we spend the time we've gained through technological advances. Rather than looking to the norms around us, why not create the norms that will nurture and nourish us?

THE WAR FOR YOUR ATTENTION

A small number of big companies, including Google, Apple, and Facebook, control what billions of us see, and how and when we see it. With algorithms, notifications, and strategic programming, these companies' decisions about how your technology works can direct your thoughts, feelings, and actions without you consciously noticing their power. This is more mass influence than any institution or religion has ever had on a group of people at one time. Sure, you might decide what to put in the search box, but you don't determine who gets to advertise a product on your screen related to your search. You may have chosen which video to watch, but not which one autoplays as soon as you finish watching, enticing you to spend more time viewing more videos.

You may love connecting, liking, and commenting with your friends on social media, but you may not have considered how every action you take online sets you up for a more alluring and addictive experience that consumes more and more of your time. Every action builds up the bank of information about your likes and dislikes, your friends and shopping habits, your demographics and location. This information then allows you to be narrowly targeted for advertising uniquely aimed at someone of your age, race, health, circumstances, profession, gender, beliefs, location, opinion, and season of life.

Designers and programmers you don't know and who don't know you are making decisions about what gets your time. They have motives that are not always in your best interest. Your time means money for the apps and websites you visit and their advertisers. Advertising dollars are set, in part, by "time on site," so the longer you engage, the more they can charge. But the human mind is adaptable. So what interested you a year ago is not enough to keep you interested today. Internet companies know this, so they continually evolve with more stimulating ways to capture your time and attention. The bar keeps getting raised, and there is no end in sight. How do they do it? Often by tapping into the natural motivations of the human mind.

We are in a battle right now, but most of us don't know it. Forces are at work, fighting ferociously for our time. The sharpest minds have been deployed to win our attention. And they have developed weapons of mass distraction. The payoff is a gold mine worth billions. Not for us—for them. We don't get a payoff, but we do pay a high price. Technology, particularly the internet and mobile apps, is deliberately designed to create a feeling of urgency that compels us to move from one activity to the next successively. Most of us have fallen prey to the lure at some point, sometimes daily. The ease of access to information means even the thought of something can lead you to search for it online; then you buy it; then an ad for a related item pops up on your news feed and you start searching for it. Before you know it, the brief thought you had has turned into a thirty-minute black hole of activity you did not plan or need to engage in. Meanwhile, the thing you meant to do remains untouched.

You may not be conscious of this war for your attention, but you certainly feel its effects: the uncontrollable urge to pick up your smartphone for no particular reason, the notification that beckons you in the middle of cooking dinner, or the electronic game you just can't seem to stop playing. Have you ever declared to yourself that you would not open up your favorite app or venture online to shop, but then your phone chimes or an ad pops up for those shoes you were browsing last week and suddenly you find yourself doing the very thing you said you wouldn't? Join the club. It is a *very big club*. Those of us who are members often struggle with borderline addictive habits that are antisocial at best and downright dangerous at worst.

Consider this story. A thirty-two-year-old woman with bright eyes, dimples, and a vibrant smile was driving down the highway headed to work. It was a good day, and she was feeling happy. So happy, in fact, that she pulled out her phone and began taking smiling selfies. She posted a status on Facebook exclaiming that the song "Happy" by Pharrell Williams made her happy. Precisely one minute after the post appeared on her Facebook page, the local police department received a call about a wreck involving her vehicle. Her car had crossed the median on the highway, slammed into a truck, and burst into flames. The driver of the truck somehow walked away unharmed. She did not. The last moment of her life was spent posting on social media while driving down the highway.[5]

I read this story several years ago, and it deeply disturbed me. Perhaps you've been the perfect driver, never distracted by a phone call, the urge to send or read a text, or the desire to look at a photo or video while driving. As ashamed as I am to admit it, I have. When I read this young woman's story, it hit me that it could have been me. It could have been someone I know and care about. It only takes one bad choice to face irreversible, devastating consequences. And for those of us who have not faced those consequences, it is not because we are any better at making choices than she was. We just happened to escape with our lives. The big question is, What compels someone to text, scroll, or post while driving? Why is it so hard for some people to wait until they are somewhere where they don't have to multitask while operating thousands of pounds of machinery moving at sixty or seventy miles an hour?

The crux of the answer is threefold:

- Personal technology today is strategically designed to capture our attention and keep it, to leave us feeling so attached to our mobile devices that some even feel drug addict–like withdrawals when they put them down.
- Our brains were developed for a world that moves slower and with less stimuli than the world we live in today. So our brains respond to threats and rewards in this modern world in predictable yet counterproductive ways.
- We have so much vying for our attention that we are forced to multitask, but by doing so, we lose our ability to distinguish what's trivial from what's important—in other words, what's meaningful versus what's a false urgency.

#MEANINGFULOVERURGENT

OLD BRAIN, NEW WORLD

To understand the significance of why it is harder than ever to reclaim your time, you must understand the brain's natural instincts.

Humans crave information deeply. It is a primitive instinct. When we get or seek information, dopamine is released in the brain. Dopamine is a neurotransmitter that helps control our brain's reward, pleasure, and reinforcement centers. When we engage in an activity that triggers the release of dopamine, it feels pleasurable, thereby enticing us to engage in that activity even more. In the grand scope of human survival, dopamine encouraged us to seek and find information because understanding the environment around us helped us survive in ancient times. Early humans had to be in constant survival mode as a matter of life and death. Gathering as much information as possible might help you notice bear tracks on the ground and avoid an attack or notice deer tracks so you could hunt the area for a good dinner.

It is instinctual to want to know as much as possible about what is going on around us. There are social rewards for having information. Our social status tends to rise when we know more than those around us. Craving information about our environment also includes the urge to know about the people around us—what they are thinking as well as what they think of us. All of this helps a person make sense of and prepare to survive in the world.

Apply this natural instinct to social media, and it becomes apparent why it can be so enticing.[6] A place to gather information about what others are doing and get affirmation about what you are doing sends regular boosts of dopamine to the brain. Social media is set up in a way that gives you concrete information about what's popular (how many likes and shares did it get?), what others think (just read the comments), and what they think of you (how many likes and comments did *you* get?). The minimal effort required to find or share ideas, articles, videos, and photos can make you feel as though you are not spending much time, when in fact the minutes are accumulating. According to a study by marketing agency Mediakix, the average person has five social media accounts, and over the course of their lifetime, will spend five years and four months on social media.[7]

Until recent history, our interactions with information and people existed in a physical realm: face-to-face, through letters or phone calls, research at the library, newspapers, and paper books. But today there is an entire world that exists electronically. The internet, mobile devices, computers, apps, websites, social media, and communication platforms are the buildings and roads, utilities and shopping centers, neighborhoods and parks of this virtual world. You can walk in and walk back out anytime you want, but the goal of every business in this virtual world is to get you to stay just a little while longer. By tapping into the natural instincts of your brain, these companies can entice you to spend more and more of your time there.

For many, the power of this virtual world is so significant that there is a rush to validate real life by constantly documenting and posting it on social media through pictures, videos, and commentary. Otherwise, did it really happen? The merging of the online world and reality can become blurred—and that means a lack of approval online can impact feelings of worthiness in real life. The investment of time to cultivate an online life that garners likes and comments can even outweigh the investment of time to cultivate meaningful moments and relationships in real life.

The boosts of dopamine we get from finding new information (a text! a social media notification! funny baby videos!) can keep us coming back for more. Dopamine drives us to do something repeatedly so that our bodies continue to release more of it. This creates a cycle of reward and reinforcement.

Dopamine also impacts our ability to focus. We typically deem things that are rewarding as worthwhile. The trap is that this is not always true, so we can find ourselves engaging in addictive behaviors for temporary moments of pleasure and motivation.

Feeling driven to gather and share information as quickly as possible helped us survive in early times, but today, in an environment in which information is limitless and instantly accessible, it can become overwhelming and even addictive. We may find ourselves acting compulsively, reaching for our smartphones for no particular reason, scanning for clues to new information—and a shot of feel-good chemicals. A University of Chicago study of 250 participants over seven days revealed that people found social media harder to resist than sex.[8] Participants admitted that yearnings to interact with comments, photos, and posts were the most difficult of all stimulants to turn down.

WEARING OUT WILLPOWER

In an environment rich with technology, resisting these urges takes a tremendous toll on our mental energy. All this temptation and reward based on basic human instincts requires a continual level of willpower previous generations have never had to exert. We are constantly making decisions about whether to answer the phone, read a text, or open an app that just sent a notification. It takes a lot of self-regulation to resist so much information available at your fingertips.

Ever been on vacation and checked your email despite declarations you wouldn't? Most white-collar workers check email on vacation; at least those in the United States do. It's hard not to. Research shows that the exertion of willpower depletes our mental energy.[9] After a series of decisions, the quality of one's decisions becomes impaired. This applies to decisions with both major and minor consequences.

OVERUSE OF TECHNOLOGY
PREVENTS DEEP THINKING

For all of the amazing good that comes from technology, it has created many challenges. One of the most consequential is the inability to think deeply about what matters and to make connections between the information we learn, according to Nicholas Carr, author of *The Shallows: What the Internet Is Doing to Our Brains*.[10] When you frequently jump from one piece of information to the next, new information does not have a chance to move from your short-term memory to your long-term memory. Short-term memory is limited, so you can hold only a small amount of information there. If you move on too quickly to new information, the information you just learned will drop from your consciousness to make room for the new before it has a chance to move to your long-term memory. Long-term memory is where information becomes knowledge. Once you've accumulated knowledge, your brain can begin making connections between knowledge to forge the understanding, creativity, and perspective that make us uniquely human.

This is the highest form of thinking of the human brain. But if you do not give your attention to anything long enough for it to transition to long-term memory, the ability to think deeply is lost. How, then, can you decide what is truly meaningful if you are unable to make these significant connections?

MULTITASKING REDUCES YOUR DECISION-MAKING ABILITY

Another noteworthy struggle is decision-making. Our brains have adapted in many ways to this modern new world of technology. In fact, most people are more efficient at changing the focus of their attention than previous generations. Multitasking is often held up as a prized skill, but it comes with a downside. According to studies at Stanford University, multitaskers fare poorly when it comes to distinguishing between trivial matters and important matters.[11]

Happiness studies confirm that something that is new or novel actually boosts feelings of positive emotion. "Interest" is a positive emotion rooted in curiosity, learning, and a sense of alertness.[12] This can, of course, be a good thing. Yet multitasking wears down your mind's ability to prioritize what is important over what is simply new or trivial. So if you've ever wondered why it is so easy to squander your time on random news articles or funny cat videos, this is one reason. When you surf from one novel video or post to the next, even though you know the project you are working on is more important, you are getting a dose of feel-good chemicals you crave.

SCREEN TIME WEARS ON YOUR BODY

"Text neck." Yep. That's what they call it when your neck becomes strained because you're looking down at your phone so much. Not the most attractive-sounding condition, is it? Like carpal tunnel syndrome that came along in the '90s, text neck is one of many side effects of screen time's wear on the body. Besides the fact that constantly tilting your head to look at a phone or sitting in front of a computer for hours per day negatively affects your posture, screen time can strain your eyes, cause headaches, and disrupt your sleep. Using your phone before bedtime has been shown to have an adverse effect on the sleep cycle due to the type of light that is emitted from the screen. Neuroscientists have concluded that the multitasking required to toggle between emails, texts, and news feeds—along with the addictive behavior that ensues—is actually rewiring our brains. Most people report feelings of anxiety when separated from their smartphones. A 2015 study showed young people performed worse on tasks when they were in "withdrawal" from their phones and experienced physiological symptoms such as increased blood pressure and heart rate, a sense of loss, and a diminishment of their extended self.[13]

When Keynes made his prediction in 1930 that we'd work just three hours a day and have abundant leisure time, he didn't foresee any of this. He imagined instead that a hundred years later, we'd use technology to lighten our loads rather than become saddled with more to-dos, an overwhelming barrage of information, and higher expectations. There's a good chance you've been distracted by texts or notifications while reading this page. You might even be reading this on your smartphone or tablet while notifications roll onto your screen with just enough interest to pique your curiosity and pry you away from your reading.

We need perspective to truly understand the impact of technology on our sense of time. The world's foremost economist could not predict accurately what technology would do to our relationship with time. He did not have the benefit of hindsight. But we do. So in the next couple of chapters, we'll step back in time to see just how we got here so that we can create an effective plan to step into a life in which we choose the meaningful over the urgent every single day.

. . . .

MEANINGFUL MINUTE

In what way is technology consuming your time more than it saves you time? How might your joy and productivity change if you regained control of that time?

_____

_____

_____

_____

CHAPTER FOUR

THE BIG BOOM

We have not always been so busy and hurried. In fact, when most of us think of times past, we envision a slower pace, more time for family and leisure, and a less demanding work schedule. So when I stumbled upon a statistic that suggests we have seven hours *more* leisure time today than we did just fifty years ago and that people a hundred and fifty years ago worked more than we work today, I was perplexed. In fact, I didn't believe it. How could this be? With so much technology and so many nonstop expectations, surely we have less spare time today for leisurely activities, right?

I began digging for other data that might prove the information wrong. What I ended up finding was more information to validate the facts: We don't work more. We have more time for leisure. But we *feel* busier and more overwhelmed than ever. This left me wondering, *Why is it that we think we are busier today than previous generations were?*

In my more than fifteen years as a personal and executive coach and positive-psychology practitioner, I've learned that curiosity is powerful. Asking the right questions helps us ultimately find meaningful answers to life's challenges. If we want to understand how we, as a society, have arrived at a point where being overwhelmed is the norm, busyness is a status symbol, and we feel naked without our phones, we must take a look at where we started and how expectations morphed over time to accommodate progress.

In the coming pages, we'll take a look at life during three specific time periods in the United States: the early 1800s, the late 1800s, and the mid-twentieth century, and in the next chapter we'll look at the acceleration of the last fifty years. By examining these periods, we'll be able to see the significance of all the progress that characterized the past two centuries and chart how that has caused our "normal" to evolve.

EARLY 1800s

Just a couple hundred years ago, the vast majority of free Americans did not work for a company or have a boss. Instead, they worked from home with family on a farm or as a skilled craftsman or a local merchant. This meant their time was under their own control. There was little pressure to be at a particular place daily at exactly the same time—well, perhaps except for the early morning cow-milking sessions. Children were educated mostly at home, so even they didn't leave home daily. Children were an important asset when it came to time because they helped with all the work that had to be done to support a family. Without a big family, it was hard to survive. Living alone as a single person was extremely rare, so family members generally stayed in the household until marriage, regardless of age. Agricultural life was demanding—and unpredictable—but it was done at home with family at a speed governed by nature. Let's go back in time and imagine what life was like and how different it truly was from life today.

As you enter into this first stop on our time-travel journey—the early 1800s—on horseback, one of the first things you notice is that there are few cities and even fewer roads connecting them. There are a little more than five million people in the United States, nearly one million of them enslaved, and fewer than one billion people around the world.[1] The American landscape is mostly trees and farmland. Towns are isolated, self-sufficient communities—islands unto themselves where residents produce their own food and make their own clothing, and skilled craftsmen earn a living making goods such as shoes and furniture. People's primary expenses are food, clothing, shelter, and work tools. They work in order to earn enough to live. And everything they need, they find locally, as transportation is both slow and expensive.

Moving from one place to another generally means walking or taking a horse. And because both of those means of transportation are slow, traveling long distances requires lots of planning. Folks and their animals will get tired. Where will they rest? They'll get hungry. What will they eat? They might also get lost. How will they find their way? Each travel obstacle requires money and time, and so traveling distances is rare. From New York, it will take a full day just to get to the outskirts of the city, two weeks to get to Ohio or Georgia, and about five weeks to get to Louisiana or Illinois. In areas where there are waterways, the river or ocean is the fastest transportation, powered by the wind.

Above all, what you notice about this stop on our journey is the pace of life. Nothing is automated or electric. The energy that moves everything is life itself: people, animals, and nature. People plant and harvest crops using the strength of animals to help them. Because nature decides the pace, there are limits to how quickly life moves. It is mostly slow and inconsistent. People get tired. Animals need rest. Wind is variable. And water ebbs and flows, freezes and melts.

People are tuned in to the rhythms of nature, in large part because time revolves around nature. It is divinely orchestrated and out of the hands of people. The cyclical rhythm of the sun determines when they rise, when they work, and when they go to sleep. The needs of their animals and crops guide their daily tasks. When the rooster crows, they wake up. When it is sowing season, they plant. When their animals need food and water, people's schedules follow those needs so that they can keep them healthy.

Everyone respects and embraces this natural rhythm and aligns their lives to make the most of the time nature allows. It is all they have ever known. Most accept it as the hand of the God who created nature and controls its pace and patterns. They even honor the sabbath principle of rest as a natural feature of their weekly ritual.

Communities are so disconnected from one another that they each keep their own time, with more than three hundred local "sun times," based on the position of the sun.[2] No one working in the fields wears a watch; clocks and personal timepieces are still very rare, individually handcrafted, and quite costly. Even in the cities and towns, you may see only a few watches owned by professionals and merchants. Most city folks use the clock at the center of town or church bells to discover the time. "I'll stop by after dinner" or "Let's meet at high noon" are description enough for most people's schedules.

LATE 1800s

As we leave behind the early 1800s, we trade our horse and buggy for a train ticket and make a stop at the turn of the twentieth century. Compared to your last mode of transportation, this ride smells better, is easier on your backside, and moves faster, but you are surrounded by strangers, and the vibration of the engine and bumpy tracks make it a little noisy. As you look out the window, you first notice how much the landscape has changed. No longer do you see a disconnected hodgepodge of independent towns and farms. Instead, you see bigger cities, smokestacks, roadways, and railways connecting a much larger country that now extends coast to coast. More and more children are leaving home to go to school. More than half of children in the late 1800s go to primary school, although attendance is much lower in rural areas and the South. Many children still also work and contribute to the welfare of the household—in factories and on the farm, as there are not yet laws regulating child labor. The American population is more than fourteen times what it was a hundred years ago. There are more than 76 million people in the United States, none legally enslaved, and there are 1.6 billion people worldwide.[3]

The domestic system that had been in existence for thousands of years and meant the whole family was involved in creating and selling products has been replaced. With the invention of the steam engine, complex machines could produce an array of products, and these advances in technology also allowed agriculture to become modernized. Cotton was at the forefront of this new system and triggered the Industrial Revolution in England as its population grew—and that opened up a trade opportunity for the United States. The domestic system of production in which people spun cloth from cotton in their homes simply could not keep up with the demand. The first textile factory was for silk, but cotton created explosive growth because it was less expensive, stronger, and easier to color and wash. The birth of cotton textile mills pulled people from rural areas into urban areas to work together in factories. With the addition of coal to power these factories, machinery could work day and night, and factory owners preferred it that way. Continuous work meant continuous money.

Cotton production increased dramatically between 1790 and 1860. In 1790, the United States produced just over three thousand bales of cotton. In 1860, the country produced nearly four million bales, primarily harvested by enslaved Americans who were motivated to find faster and faster ways of working in order to avoid harsh treatment.[4] Their efficiency coupled with textile manufacturing advances that allowed more cotton to be produced and exported transformed the United States in under a hundred years from an almost exclusively agrarian society to the leading industrialized nation in the entire world. Cotton is king at this point in time, but it has plenty of company: steel, iron, agriculture, and more.

The American Industrial Revolution of the late nineteenth century didn't just revolutionize business; it was a *time revolution*. A new era has now reshaped how daily life is structured. Starting at this point in history, time is no longer governed by nature. It is not dependent on the sun. There is electricity, so work hours are not limited to natural daylight. Work is also no longer restrained by the needs of people, who must take breaks because they need to eat or sleep. Machines run 24-7 in factories that never close. No longer is time bound by slow-paced animals needed to power work on the farm. Instead, coal and steam engines supply power nonstop. The machines never get tired. And no longer is transportation limited to horses and buggies. A system of railroads from New York to California means that traveling three thousand miles no longer takes months, but only four days.

With new sources of energy and new machines, the speed of work has reached a pace never seen before. This dramatically impacts the lives of working people. Just take a look inside a typical urban factory and you'll see workers focused and intense. They are paid by the hour and must continually produce at a level that meets the production goals of the factory. A whistle blows and they stop work. It's time for a quick break to eat.

No one leaves the building. Instead, you see them grab their lunch boxes, eat together, and chat a bit. The foods they have packed are unusual for this time of day compared to a century ago when dinner was a hot meal—the biggest of the day—eaten in the early afternoon. Lunch is an invention of the Industrial Revolution, and workers can no longer prepare a big midday meal and eat at home. It must be quick and portable. As you watch the workers open their metal lunch boxes, you see pie, biscuits, and a popular new phenomenon: sandwiches—all time-conscious lunch options. When the whistle blows again, it's back to work.

Work is no longer about producing a product start to finish and selling it to earn a living. Instead, these workers are selling their time. Hours are long, and breaks are minimal. And children work, too, just as they had on the farm. Six-day workweeks are the norm. To be clear, their grandparents and great-grandparents worked long hours on the farm, typically from sunup until sundown with very little spare time. But these workers no longer have control over the scheduling of their work lives. Someone else decides that.

This is the reality for more and more people at the turn of the century. Due to industrial advances, there are fewer farmers. And because factories are manufacturing products faster and more cheaply than a skilled craftsman ever could, earning a living in agriculture and skilled trades has become harder than ever. For millions in rural areas, it's a surer financial bet to move to the city and trade your time for money.

Such was the case in my own family as they sought a better way of life. My paternal grandparents—the ones I spent my summers with—were sharecroppers, farmers who were cheated out of their earnings by the landowner whose land they worked. My grandmother was stout and energetic, with a wide smile that greeted pretty much everyone she saw. Granddaddy was humble, never missed a day of work even on Saturdays, and was smart despite having dropped out of school in the fifth grade to help his family in the fields.

The last year they sharecropped, the landowner cheated them so badly, Grandmama told me that Granddaddy stormed back home fuming mad. With little recourse for getting the money they were owed without endangering their lives, they decided it was time to do something else for a living. That's when my grandparents moved from their rural town of several hundred people to the county seat, a city of nineteen thousand where textile factories and mills were the primary employer. Granddaddy went to work for J. P. Stevens & Company, a textile manufacturer, and Grandmama became a domestic and later an elementary school cook and dietitian. Like many country folk of their era, they transitioned from rural life to city life, albeit small-city life. And with city life, especially for a factory worker, time is a tyrant.

Factories are on a schedule, and to accommodate the demands of business, so is everyone else. With railroads and steam engines, products that were once produced and sold locally can be produced anywhere, then marketed and transported where they are needed. But this requires massive coordination. Timing must be precise—and it must be nationalized.

The self-sustaining, independent communities of previous generations cannot hold their ground against the tide of progress. Having three hundred–plus time zones simply will not work any longer. So in 1883, a nationalized system of standard time zones is created.[5] This system is also aligned with an international system created in England to address the same challenge.

The management and coordination of a massive production system also means there must be lots of communication. The latest gadgets, such as typewriters, telephones, carbon paper, and adding machines, have been invented to gather, share, disseminate, and record information as quickly and efficiently as possible.

So what does all of this production mean for individuals? Suddenly, time matters more than ever, because it is dictated by the demands of business. People's work schedules are determined by their bosses and organized in shifts. Transportation is advanced and runs on a tight schedule. There are more people than ever before, and life is moving faster than ever before. Time is no longer a natural, divinely orchestrated rhythm, unpredictable and slow, but an undeniable force orchestrated by the manmade demands of industry that is precise, regimented, and fast-paced.

Just as significant is the direct connection now made between *time* and *money.* With an hourly wage now the standard, people are no longer worried about their crops failing or if there is enough demand for their shoemaking, carpentry, or dressmaking skills. What they sell now is their time. With time as a commodity, it feels scarcer, and how it is spent becomes more consequential.

MID-1900s

If it seems mind-boggling to consider how our personal time was impacted due to the changes that occurred between 1800 and 1900, the next hundred years are even more stunning. Between 1900 and 1950, the US population has doubled from 76 million to just over 152 million, and the world population has grown to 2.5 billion.[6] Young people are spending much more time in school and much less time working or starting families. With the movement toward secondary education in the first half of the century, a high school diploma is now the norm for eighteen-year-olds. Four more years are spent on formal education than was the case just a few decades earlier.

Rather than by train, as we did on our last stop, let's make our stop in the mid-twentieth century in an automobile. There are millions of these vehicles on the road now, and it has transformed how people live, where they live, and how fast they live. As you cruise down the brand-new interstate highways that cross the country, the cities look bigger and more spread out than ever. And there are more cities, big and small. The distinction is no longer simply between "rural" and "urban." In fact, as you land in one of the cities, you hear someone mention that they live in the "suburbs"—an abbreviation of the new term *suburban* that has recently emerged to describe the sprawl of cities that have become large metropolitan areas. Lots of people who work in the city no longer live in the city. Instead, they live on the outskirts.

Large cities are booming; in fact, most of the ten largest cities in the United States before 1950 are at their peak and will see population declines in the coming decades.[7] Cars have made the suburbs possible, and the suburbs mean cars are now a necessity. Just a few decades ago, people who worked in the city lived nearby, but today that's unnecessary. The automobile allows people to live far from work and commute distances that were previously impossible—which adds significant time to the process of going to and coming from work.

Four major advances, in particular, are transforming everyone's perceptions and expectations about time: broadcast communication, the telephone, air travel, and the automobile.

Let's first talk about the automobile, which changed the country's physical landscape. Although the first automobile was created in the late 1800s, it was the 1930s before they became affordable for the growing middle class. By the time the famous Ford Model T, the first mass-produced personal automobile, was withdrawn from production in 1927, 15 million had been sold, and the price was under $300 (just under $4,127 in today's dollars)—about one-third of what it cost when it was launched nearly two decades earlier.[8] Buyers were given the option to buy "on time," meaning they could make payments over time to pay for a vehicle, a previously uncommon practice. Between 1950 and 1958, the number of registered automobiles would more than double to 67 million.[9]

The ability to move more quickly through the world not only impacts the distance between work and home but also people's expectations about convenience and speed. Drive-through restaurants and theaters abound. Starting in 1955, the federal government invests in the development of a system of interstate highways that links together cities and towns across the United States with wide, multilane highways that allow people to travel at high speeds with no stops.

As you cruise along the interstate, though, you notice something else: billboards. In this new era, the art of mass marketing is reaching an all-time high, changing people's expectations about what they ought to have and how much. If time is money, spending just a little more time could get you more of what you want, right? One of the most persistent marketing strategies of the twentieth century emerged from the automobile industry.

With so many cars on the road by the 1920s, demand for replacement cars slowed. This led to a practice, first initiated by General Motors under the leadership of Alfred P. Sloan, that continues to influence our buying and timing habits to this day. Sloan declared that the primary purpose of the manufacturer was not to make cars, but to make money. So he pioneered a strategy called "planned obsolescence." The idea was to make automobile owners discontented with their cars by making styling and technology changes on an annual basis that made a car buyer's existing car "obsolete." So by the 1950s, although cars are made in much the same way as they were thirty years earlier, car-buying demand is as swift as ever. You might not need a new car—your car works just fine—but that doesn't mean you don't *want* the latest, greatest model. The strategy allows GM to eclipse Ford and remain the leading car manufacturer for the next six decades.

Whereas in the pre-industrial era, most individuals were focused on earning enough to live and get what they needed by bartering in addition to spending money, twentieth-century expectations about what is required to live shift more from "need" to "want." With billboards and soon television, advertising has grown into a full-fledged adult and given birth to conspicuous consumption, a phenomenon that drives us to work and spend more.

But the highway isn't the only place people are exposed to advertising messages. Cars have radios, and radio stations sell advertising. There is an increased and constant exposure to ideas beyond people's immediate environment. Advertising is everywhere, and suddenly people are seeing things they didn't even know they wanted. But broadcast communication is also about to explode with a new technology. Peer into the living room of the average family after dinner in the mid-twentieth century, and you are likely to see parents and children gathered around a television set.

Early twentieth-century labor laws dramatically decreased work schedules to cut down on industry abuses of workers, and new technologies such as washing machines and dryers, indoor plumbing, and personal automobiles, are saving people lots of time. Time-use records show that people during this period have more leisure time than at any point in this century. And much of it is spent watching television. This new form of entertainment is so popular it sometimes even alters daily schedules. Families don't even need to stop to eat dinner. The invention of the "TV dinner" is introduced in 1954, allowing people to pop a meal into the oven and watch their favorite show while they eat.

There's one more innovation that has sped up time: commercial flying becomes common by the late 1950s. With nonstop, transcontinental flights, what used to be considered a luxury is now another reliable mode of transportation that cuts travel time from days to hours. A job opportunity in California might seem unthinkable if it takes eight days of roundtrip travel to visit your family on the East Coast. But if it is a mere five-hour flight each way, suddenly your options have expanded. Your world just got smaller.

With all of these advances—air travel, personal automobiles, and broadcast communication—life's basic needs have become increasingly less basic and more costly. The time revolution of the last two hundred years moved us from a natural rhythm to a precise and man-made pace powered by technology. It changed everything about how we live, even making it in some ways harder to be happy. In the last fifty years, culture and technology changes have accelerated. As a result, time tyranny, which is the constant pull to cram more activities into smaller amounts of time, has grown stronger, making it harder than ever to loosen its grip. First, let's talk about the changes. Then we'll uncover how it all affects us and the hope we have for living life in a way that reflects our deepest craving for meaning and joy.

MEANINGFUL MINUTE

What can you do to remind yourself of the need to pause and disconnect from the accelerated pace of modern life?

_____

_____

_____

_____

CHAPTER FIVE

HOW CHANGING TIMES HAVE CHANGED OUR TIME

W hen is enough enough and you get to enjoy getting to where you wanted to be?" Allison asked, reflecting on an event she'd attended that morning where everyone seemed to be striving for the next level. A stay-at-home mom for the past eighteen years, she is just moving into a new season of life as her youngest has headed off to college. Now she's building a home-based business but doesn't want it to consume all of her time. "It just seems like I don't meet anyone who isn't trying to climb to another level, even if they've been at it for years. Is it okay to have a goal, and once you get to it, just enjoy it and be excellent at it? Do we always have to spend time reaching for something more?"

Her question tugged at me, as I have often asked a similar question—and coached others to answer it. As we consider the changes in our culture over the last half century, one of the unexpected themes that emerges is how they affect our happiness. Note that what has become normal collides with many of the factors known to contribute to happiness: strong relationships, family, community, connection, faith, and financial stability. As these foundations of happiness have weakened and the demands of time have multiplied, the quest for happiness has become more elusive.

Since the 1960s, in fact, standards of living have doubled, but happiness levels have not.[1] This is true in the United States as well as in countries such as Great Britain and Japan. One persistent myth is that success causes happiness, but research shows that the truth is the other way around: happiness causes success.[2] We pursue most everything else in life because we believe it will make us happier. So the incessant drive to "get to the next level"—to be "successful"—is often a quest for meaning and happiness in a modern world that makes both more challenging to find. This is not to say we should never spend our time striving for success, but to find happiness, that striving must hold meaning.

Take a moment right now to think about your top goal in life. What will achieving it give you that you don't already have? In other words, what makes it worth spending your time to pursue it?

MORE OPPORTUNITY, BUT LESS HAPPINESS

Two major shifts occurred in the last half century that have brought us to a cultural and technological revolution that impacts our relationship with time. First, the shift in opportunities for women not only changed the dynamic of the family unit that has been the foundation of society but also created ripples that affect everything from household demographics, debt, and inflation to education, gender roles, and the happiness levels of both men and women. Second, advancements in technology have sped up the pace of life and the volume of information we must process every single day.

Little by little, these changes have led us to a place of overwhelming options, relentless time pressure, and a craving for community in a hyperconnected world. We all feel it, and often we are at a loss about what to do about it. It is nearly impossible to live in today's society and not experience the effects. Daily life is easier and more comfortable, cleaner, and more convenient than at any other time in history. Yet the pace and expectations of modern life have created a convergence of circumstances that make life satisfaction and contentment harder to achieve. Research shows that while happiness levels have not increased, rates of depression have doubled. Women are twice as likely as men to be depressed, and the first onset of depression is younger than ever.

Women today have more money, more education, and better health than forty years ago. We live longer, have higher graduation rates, and in many instances, better job prospects than men. And we have more protections than our mothers and grandmothers did— from sexual harassment policies to domestic violence laws. But in spite of these gains, a perplexing trend began happening around 1972. Whereas women in the 1960s and before reported higher levels of happiness than men, over the last several decades, it seems it is men's happiness that's gotten a boost while women's happiness moved in the opposite direction. Men and women had also both reported higher happiness levels as they aged, but starting in 1972, women in mid-life began to see happiness decline.[3]

A groundbreaking paper, "The Paradox of Declining Female Happiness," from economists Betsey Stevenson and Justin Wolfers of the University of Pennsylvania's Wharton School of Business, revealed that women today, especially starting in their early forties, feel less satisfied with their lives than women a half century ago did. The researchers found these trends hold true across industrialized nations regardless of how women are spending their time—whether they do or don't work outside of the home; whether they are single, married, or divorced; and whether or not they are mothers.

These findings also hold true across races, except for the one exception: African American women, whose happiness levels continue to rise, but who still report less happiness than African American men. African American women were already working outside the home in much greater numbers than other groups before the early 1970s, and during that time period, they began to see some positive residual effects of the civil rights movement in terms of better job opportunities and fairer treatment.

The paper used data from the annual US General Social Survey, but similar results appear in at least six other major studies in the United States and countries around the globe.[4]

With more women working, earning four-year and graduate degrees, and contributing to or leading their households, we have added time-consuming, pressure-filled responsibilities but have let go of very few of the responsibilities we already had.[5] Don't get me wrong. Men are doing much more household work than in previous generations, but women still do the majority of it. And we tend to carry the never-ending, invisible workload of "household and family manager," a job we used to call housewife or homemaker. If this is one of your jobs, the to-do list is nonstop. *Are we running out of cereal? Did I remember to put my child's uniform in the dryer before work so that it's clean for the game tonight? Has the permission slip for the school field trip made it into the backpack for tomorrow? Did I check the calendar and RSVP to my cousin's wedding invitation? Have I ordered a gift? It's time for the six-month dental checkups. When can I get a break to call and make them?*

Individually, these types of tasks may seem small, but together, they are relentless. They don't just take up time. They take up bandwidth—the sheer number of things you are handling at one time. And then there are the big things: holiday planning, family celebrations, and coordinating some sort of social life, all of which are a part of the invisible workload too. It is a lot to keep up with for someone with no other job. With a job, it gets chaotic. And because women are more likely to worry, the threat of dropping the ball creates anxiety and chronic exhaustion. Nonetheless, household and family tasks have to get done, and the time must come from somewhere. So when it feels like there is no other option, we steal the time from other areas of life—areas we'd rather maintain because they are meaningful.

Happiness is largely a product of expectations. As times have changed, what has changed about our time is that we have much higher expectations about how much we should be able to do with the finite time we have. As women have gained more options in recent decades, there is more opportunity for second-guessing our choices, more opportunity for regret. The woman who chooses to stay at home may often wonder if she's made the right choice by opting out of the workforce, creating a gap in her work experience she may never be able to compensate for if and when she wants or needs to work in the future. The woman who has decided to climb the corporate ladder or run a business may sometimes long to be at home, especially if she has growing children. The pull, the guilt, and the doubt can all be a drain on happiness. With heightened expectations about what life should look like, influenced by a greater awareness of others' lives through television, social media, and advertising, the problem may not be that we are less happy. The problem may be that we have higher expectations about what we should be able to accomplish and the timeline by which we should accomplish it.

THE RISE OF THE DUAL-INCOME FAMILY

After World War II, just 10 percent of mothers with children under the age of six worked outside of the home. By 1985, the US Census showed more than half of mothers of children under the age of six worked. By 2017, the number was 65 percent (and 75 percent for mothers with children aged six to seventeen).[6]

Think for a moment about the changes that enabled large numbers of dual-income families. In the early twentieth century, the idea of two parents working outside the home on a daily basis was much harder to imagine. Washing clothes, cooking, and child care were all time-intensive tasks. Before microwaves, pre-cut vegetables, and fast-food on every corner, meals were cooked from scratch and took hours to prepare. Day care centers and preschools were nonexistent.

When women entered the workforce en masse in the 1970s, there was one big perk: these new two-parent families saw a major boost to their bank accounts. With inflation rising as well as consumption, it was becoming harder to support a comfortable, middle-class lifestyle on one income. With prolific advertising and mass marketing of products broadcasting on television into the living rooms of 95 percent of households by 1970 (up from just 9 percent in 1950),[7] consumerism was growing. Whether the intention was boosting household income or giving the woman of a household the opportunity to pursue a professional life, families began trading more of their time for money. And that trend persisted.[8]

As the decades have progressed, the impact of women's financial earnings on household income has grown. Two-earner couples today make 23 percent more than two-earner couples in 1970. A 2015 Pew research survey of dual-income families showed that the average couple with two full-time earners makes six figures: $102,400 per year.[9] These couples make up nearly half of two-parent households, up from 31 percent in 1970. Their single-income counterparts in which one parent stays home while the other works? Their annual income is about half of that: $55,000. Single-income families make up just 26 percent of two-parent households today, half the proportion they comprised in 1970. And survey data shows specifically that if the father works full-time and the mother works part-time, the median income is about $84,000.[10]

The thing is, all that extra money is not free. It costs time—lots of it: more than two thousand hours per year for full-time workers, plus the time preparing for and traveling to and from work. With an average daily commute time of about fifty minutes, add another three hundred–plus hours per year for the commute, and you can see why two-earner couples are stretched thin. Significant numbers say they struggle with work-life balance, are stressed, and feel hurried daily. So while their earning potential is much greater, allowing for a higher standard of living and expensive perks, they pay for it with time spent away from home, family, and leisure activities. I know this reality well. Designing a life that includes meaningful work for both spouses, financial security, and a healthy family life takes work and a willingness to be flexible and creative. Maybe one of you has the dominant career for a period of time, or one opts out of the job market during critical seasons in your family, or you both find jobs that are fulfilling, but not as demanding as other options. The key is taking the time to think it through, decide what really matters, and chart a course that makes sense for your family even if it doesn't look like the norms around you.

THE EMERGENCE OF THE ONE-PERSON HOUSEHOLD

Another of the most significant demographic changes of the modern era is the rise of the one-person household. Though it was nearly impossible in pre-industrial times and still rare even in the 1960s, today more and more people live alone. If you're not one of them, I bet you know quite a few. Consider this: A century ago, just 6 percent of households consisted of one person. By 1940, that number was still less than 8 percent of all households. In 2013, it was 28 percent—more than 35 million households. There are significantly more one-person households today than there are married couples with minor children at home.[11]

In times past, the overwhelming majority of one-person households were men, they were renters, and it was a short-term living arrangement—often a transition stage between single life and marriage. But today, the majority of these households are women (54 percent), they own their homes (also 54 percent), and it is a long-term living arrangement.[12]

So what are the factors that led to an increase in the number of one-person households? First, changes in economic norms and social values shifted demographics and preferences. More economic opportunities for women since the 1970s have led to expanded financial choices. Marriage is no longer the primary path to financial security for women. Even among women who want marriage, those who go to college and have successful careers often find that dream deferred. The availability of birth control beginning in the 1960s allowed for the delay of starting a family. It was also one of the reasons sex outside of marriage became more common and less taboo.

Then in 1970, California became the first state to introduce the no-fault divorce, allowing couples to dissolve a marriage without proving wrongdoing by either party. As of 2010, when New York passed its no-fault divorce law, every state in the United States had the law—and seventeen states no longer allow fault-based grounds to be alleged in divorce court.[13] These legal changes led to a big uptick in divorce, resulting in many more single adults who at an earlier era in history may have been forced to stay married.

All of these changes converge to create more one-person households, and while many love living alone, it is a definite shift in individual time pressure. The responsibilities of running a household fall to one person rather than two, literally leaving them with half as much time to do the things required to run a household.

I was single for all of my twenties and the last few years of my thirties. There are definite advantages and freedoms that come with being single. Last-minute plans were a cinch. I cooked only if I felt like it, and if I didn't, Rice Krispies were an acceptable dinner choice. I look back wistfully at the days when I did laundry once every one to two weeks. Now, if I don't do laundry every other day, I risk a pile so big I might end up buried alive in the laundry room.

But one very real challenge to being single is this: doing everything yourself. Whether it is staying on top of the finances, getting chores done, or planning social activities, saving time by sharing the responsibility with a spouse is not an option. Staying home instead of working a job is also not an option, unless you have a trust fund or pension, or are independently wealthy. When you're going it alone, running and supporting a household falls entirely in your lap. That means more pressure on your time. Pressure to succeed. Pressure to manage everything yourself. And if the goal is to be married at some point, pressure to be a desirable prospective mate—to be social and be seen, look your best, and manage dating relationships all take up time.

DIVORCE AND THE SINGLE-PARENT HOUSEHOLD

The other single-income household that has grown exponentially in modern times is the single-parent household. Many divorcées are parents, and this is the group with perhaps *the most* time pressure of all. Not only do they deal with managing the entire household alone, like the millions of single-person households that have emerged in recent decades, but they also bear sole responsibility for the day-to-day care and raising of children. Even when custody is shared, they do not have in-the-moment support from the other parent on the days they care for their kids. If there is a last-minute challenge upon waking up in the morning, there's no rolling over to a spouse to say, "Hey, can you take them to school this morning?" If you are sick, the children still need to be fed, homework still needs to be done, and bills still need to be paid.

Mine was one of those families in the late twentieth century that didn't make it out intact. My parents separated just before I started high school. For two years of high school, I lived with my father, and the second two years, I lived with my mother.

We had been a dual-income household. My father enlisted in the US Air Force not long before I was born, and my mother was a stay-at-home mom until I started first grade. They went to college while working and raising me and eventually were able to enhance their professional opportunities. If there was any stress about money before my parents' separation, I didn't feel it. They had built our home in a middle-class subdivision in a sought-after school district in suburban Denver. I remember we spent months shopping for just the right furniture to furnish it as nicely as the sales models at the front of the neighborhood.

When my parents separated, everything changed. Although I had come home to an empty house after school every day because both of my parents worked, after their separation I found myself home by myself longer as both of my parents took on additional part-time jobs in the evenings to stay afloat now that there were two separate households—sometimes leaving for work before I got up for school and getting home after I went to sleep.

My dad somehow managed to make it to my track and gymnastics meets on weekends, and my mom was an enthusiastic supporter of my modeling and pageant aspirations. But their time was limited. Frankly, I don't know how they did it. Reminiscing on that time now, they both have told me they simply did what they had to do, and they explain that there really wasn't much time to bemoan their circumstances. That's what millions of single parents do.

Regardless of the circumstances that lead to single parenthood, there is no denying that it is the group most pressed for time. And there are more people who fall into this group than ever.

LUXURIES BECOME NECESSITIES AND DEBT FUELS THE SHIFT

Modern life has brought with it so many luxuries. But have you ever stopped to really think about how all of these luxuries create financial, and therefore, time demands? We live lives our ancestors could only dream of. But it is easy not to notice that so much of what is a necessity today (or at least feels like one) was a luxury when it was introduced— electricity, cars, telephones, and television, to name a few. Technology is big business. As new technology makes life more convenient and efficient, the acquisition of such technology costs money—and for most people, that means it costs more time.

When people compare households of today to households fifty years ago, it is often in a nostalgic way and with the assumption that a dual income is necessary in order to live the same lifestyle as a one-income household a half century ago. In reality, the comparison often discounts the significance of our collective rise in expectations and norms.

Today's families have many expenses that were simply non-existent in the mid-twentieth century, chief among them the gizmos and gadgets that we rely on for communication, education, and entertainment. Add to that the prospect of saving for retirement in a world of smaller, geographically disconnected families, few pensions, and longer life expectancy. Generation Xers are the first 401(k) generation, and along with Millennials, can expect to fund their own retirements rather than relying on pensions, which were common for previous generations. But we aren't doing it. Thirty-four percent of

Gen Xers and 39 percent of Millennials have zero saved for retirement.[14] We can expect a future in which retirement takes longer to get to and far more effort to achieve. Simply put, most people will spend more years working—unless they have an aggressive plan of action for earning and saving. The result will be more years in the workforce, more time spent caring for elders, and more pressure on the children of older adults because they had fewer children than previous generations. It is a frightening reality, one we should have an action plan to avoid.

During the first stop on our time travel journey in the last chapter, the early 1800s, basic expenses included food, clothing, shelter, and work tools, all of which were often produced by a family or purchased locally. After the Industrial Revolution and up until the 1950s, expenses that started out as luxuries, like indoor plumbing and electric lighting, became necessities. Other expenses included rent, twenty- to thirty-year mortgages, car payments, car insurance, and gasoline. In the late twentieth century, more luxuries morphed into necessities for modern life: personal computers, televisions, cell phones, cable/satellite/streaming television, and internet. The bottom line? It is more expensive to live in modern society because we adapt to progress, and technological progress is typically tied to products and services that cost us money. Sure, you could decide to forgo the "modern necessities," but you would be isolated from people, opportunities, and the reality of how the world works today. Your life would be harder. Applying for a job or running a business would be nearly impossible. Communicating with friends and family would be limited, especially if they don't live nearby. You could write and mail letters, but it's slow, and would anyone take the time to write you back?

One of the biggest examples of luxury-turned-necessity is the mobile phone. The first cell phone, the Motorola DynaTAC, was sold to a consumer in the early 1980s. It was thirteen inches long, the battery drained in about thirty minutes, and it was so heavy it was affectionately called "The Brick." It was rare to see one. It was expensive. But above all, it was a status symbol. It cost the equivalent of three months' salary for the average American—$3,995.[15] It was definitely a luxury in the 1980s, and arguably into the 1990s. But as the size and price of phones dropped and more consumers purchased them, they moved from luxury to necessity. Today, more than 95 percent of adults own a cell phone,[16] and many of them have cell phones for their kids too. For more than half of adults, a mobile device is their only phone, as they no longer have a landline at home.

What was once a luxury is now pretty much a necessity that eats up more than $1,200 of the average family's annual household budget.[17] Mobile phones, of course, are not the only luxury that has become a necessity. One late-twentieth-century change that has enabled many of the necessities of modern life is debt.

"MORE STUFF, MORE DEBT" BECOMES A NEW NORMAL

People began shifting their attitudes toward personal debt about fifty years ago—and that shift occurred *relative to* the financial behavior of the collective group. It is perfectly illustrated by a popular commercial for the loan company Lending Tree in the early 2000s. You might even remember it.

The commercial showed a dazed, smiling man grilling in his suburban backyard and introducing his lovely wife and three, well-groomed kids, then ticking off a list of his prized achievements. "I've got a great family," he says, squeezing them all tightly as they smile for the camera. "I've got a four-bedroom house in a great community," he proclaims while leaning against the lovely fireplace in his perfectly decorated living room. "Like my car?" he asks in the next scene with a forced smile while driving his shiny SUV through his neighborhood.

"It's new." Then we see him on the golf course with friends, and he says with a nod and a whisper, "I even belong to the local golf club."

"How do I do it?" he asks rhetorically while cleaning his backyard pool as his family plays in the background. "I'm in debt up to my eyeballs!" He pauses. "I can barely pay my finance charges," he says in a daze as he continues the fake smile while driving his shiny, new riding lawnmower. "Somebody help me," he whimpers as the commercial closes and he haphazardly drives the lawnmower off track and toward the sidewalk.[18]

It's hard trying to keep up with the Joneses.

Many people realize something is amiss, aware that much of what they've committed to isn't out of desire to commit to it but because it is the norm—what everyone else is doing. If they are all doing it, it must be what I should do, too, right?

Until the 1950s, the idea of borrowing money on a credit card was mostly unheard of. The first charge card, Diners Club, was introduced in 1950. Primarily for entertainment and dining purposes, the card had to be paid in full each month. Other companies came along with cards, too, but the purpose of these services was primarily convenience, not financial need.

Then in 1958, Bank of America introduced the BankAmericard. It was the first revolving credit card. For a small finance charge, you could now carry a balance each month and make a minimum payment. This new product created a shift in thinking and changed how consumers shopped—and ultimately altered their expectations about what was possible.

I want you to pause for a moment and imagine a world in which consumers, you included, could only buy what they had saved up to purchase. How would that limit what you could afford? How would it change your monthly expenses? And how would that impact the time you must spend earning money to cover those expenses? A client of mine and her husband decided to make adjustments to live this way and, within a few years, were semi-retired in their early 40s. Their cars are older and their comfortable, modest home in an affordable midwestern city is now paid in full. It took a lot of discipline, but they reclaimed their time by downsizing their lifestyle.

The idea of borrowing is now woven into the fabric of our economy. The new normal is to borrow decades into your future. In essence, financial debt leads to time debt, as the borrower promises future income—mostly gained by the spending of their time to earn it. With stagnant wages and rising expenses, the idea of finding some sort of freedom can feel daunting. And the things you invested your time and finances acquiring have led to short-term happiness and long-term stress and worry as years of fiscal and temporal commitment lie ahead.

People take their cues from one another in a process called *relative consumption*. As those around you raise their standard of living and buy more luxuries and goods, their behavior becomes the norm. But when you do the same, it doesn't bring you more happiness. If your satisfaction comes from having the same or more than those around you, then there is never a limit to how much you need in order to be satisfied. Relative consumption creates a race with no finish line. At some point, you must make a decision to get out of the race and intentionally choose what is meaningful over what feels urgent just because it is the norm around you.

SO WHAT DOES ALL THIS MEAN FOR YOU?

So much of what has happened in the last half century has been positive progress, but the way these changes have manifested in our everyday lives impacts our time and happiness:

- We have more opportunities, but that hasn't necessarily led to more happiness. To choose what is meaningful is to evaluate every opportunity and ask yourself if it holds meaning for you that is truly worthy of your time and attention. You may be surprised to discover your answers.

- The rise of dual-income and single-person households has left more people struggling with time tyranny. Get clear about your long-term vision, the help you might need, and whether you want to make major lifestyle changes that give you more time for what matters most.
- Luxuries have become necessities. Notice the things that have shifted from one to the other; then decide whether you want them to remain necessities, counting the cost and time required to maintain such expenses.
- More stuff, more debt. Although debt has become the norm, you don't have to resign yourself to a life in which debt is a permanent fixture, and therefore a main driver in how much time you spend earning money to alleviate your debt.

Research has shown that strong relationships, a sense of community, faith, connection, and financial comfort all correlate with happiness, but the changes over the last fifty years have led to less time and focus on each of these. The feeling of being overwhelmed and overloaded did not happen overnight. By peeling back the layers of change, we can begin to understand what's happened, and we can start to put our finger on the paradox of free time in which climbing the ladder of success no longer means having a life with more leisure or even more happiness, but instead a life in which we feel continually compelled to do more.

MEANINGFUL MINUTE

In what ways has your own life story been impacted by the changes that have become the new normal over the last half century (debt, dual-income or single-person/single-parent household, more opportunity)?

_____

_____

_____

How have these norms impacted your time?

_____

_____

_____

CHAPTER SIX

MAKING PEACE
WITH LOST TIME

One of the consequences of living in a way that allows false urgencies to drive our decisions is that we hyperfocus on the present without looking up to consider a future created by our present-day choices. This takes reflection. It takes intention. It takes planning. And it requires the kind of deep thinking made difficult by the tech-rich environment in which we live, where a focus on speed and checking off boxes often outweighs a meaningful, deliberate approach. Whether the decision is relational or financial, physical or professional, in order to choose what is meaningful, you must recognize the value of time—your time, in particular.

Your time is a finite resource. Once it's gone, you cannot reclaim it. And unlike money, no one can generously hand over their extra time to you as a gift. You cannot work more to earn more hours in the day. You cannot negotiate to relive that year that didn't go so well. Like money, though, if you don't value your time, you are much more likely to make choices that end up wasting it. You'll say yes to situations that deserve more thoughtful consideration before making a commitment.

Remember saving up money when you were a child? Maybe it was birthday money or money earned babysitting, and when you finally had enough to make a big purchase, it was exciting. You began thinking about what you wanted to do with your cash. And if you saved a decent amount, the stakes were high. You wanted to make the right decision because you knew once you spent it, it would take a lot of time and effort to accumulate that much money again. You weighed all of your options, and when you finally made a purchase, you treasured your new prized possession. It was off-limits to siblings. You guarded it and took great care of it.

That is the behavior of someone who values the money they've accumulated and what they choose to spend it on. What if we valued our time in that way, truly appreciating it as a gift and protectively choosing how to spend it?

Too often we do just the opposite. We don't carefully consider the value of time. And so, when major decisions are at stake, we fail to consider the consequences of choosing poorly. We rush decisions about relationships, too quickly take on debt that will require years to pay off, and put off appointments and get-togethers with the assumption we'll have time to get to them later. Meanwhile, we give our time to activities that feel urgent in the moment, but don't have a lasting impact. We make decisions based on socially or self-imposed timelines about the milestones of life—it's time to get married, time to have kids, time to buy a house or new car—even when we aren't at peace about whether it is indeed the time for us personally to move toward such milestones.

The consequence is landing at a place you never meant to be and realizing you've lost time you cannot reclaim. Some dreams have a window of opportunity, and once missed, it is forever closed. Time, after all, *is* life. And some seasons change before we are ready. Perhaps you've been there. I certainly have. This was a hard-learned lesson for me.

THE STING OF LOST TIME

Have you ever felt the sting of lost time you'll never get back? The loss brings a sorrow that is haunting. I have never felt a pain so palpable yet intangible as that of wanting to reach back and reclaim the six childbearing years I lost in a marriage that didn't make it.

As one chapter of my life closed and a new and uncertain one began, my heart stung with the bitter reality. The long journey of healing, finding true love, marrying again, and bearing children would likely outlast the ticking of my biological clock. I desperately wanted those years back. Yet nothing I could do would ever grant that wish.

For a while, I felt like I'd had the emotional wind knocked out of me. My thoughts spiraled. I anxiously did mental math on my biological clock. The results were painful and deeply distressing as I added up the years it could take if I held out hope for my personal dreams of a future that included a happy marriage and children. My thoughts were like two versions of me battling it out: the faith-filled me and the fear-filled me, plodding and guessing, hoping and fearing, methodically and logically adding up the years to figure out if my dream was still a possibility:

> Let's see, I'm thirty-six. The divorce will take a year. It'll probably take two years just to work through this pain I feel and really heal so I don't end up back here ever again.
>
> Then there's meeting somebody. Oh geez. I hadn't even thought about that process. Wait a minute. I'm going to have to date again? I hate dating! I don't want to date. Ugh. I. Do. Not. Like. Dating.
>
> Okay. Pull it together. I know you are not looking forward to it, but you'll have to date for a while. Maybe a couple of years before you meet the right one. And at that point, let's say you are three years down the road and you meet him—the one. And then y'all will need some time together before you decide to get married.

#MEANINGFULOVERURGENT

So let's see. Two years of healing, two years to meet the one, a year or two dating each other. We are at five to six years. At that point you're in your early forties. You can still have children then, right?

Maybe. But if this math doesn't work out just right, it might not happen.

Don't say that.

It might not.

It could.

Do you have faith or don't you?

I have faith, but it hurts to hope when the path looks so narrow . . .

The experience of missing your window of opportunity, falling behind, or regretting decisions can create an anxiety that unconsciously rules your relationship with time. Whether it is the relationship you now regret staying in for too long, the way you wish you'd just stuck it out and finished your education, or past financial choices that left you working harder than ever to catch up to where you think you should be by now, the feelings are real.

I felt as if my hands were stretched toward the past, hoping to grab hold of it and somehow recapture the time. Thinking back, the time felt so recent. It was right there. And yet it was gone forever.

So what happens when time slips out of your hands? When there is a real ticking clock that will eventually run out? Thinking in very stark terms about what it means to lose time can help you value it more deeply and ultimately make future decisions more intentionally. In what ways have you lost time?

MAKING PEACE WITH LOST TIME

If you have struggled with lost time in any area of your life, I invite you to first have a bit of compassion for yourself. It can be tempting to beat yourself up, to wallow in regret, or to get trapped in a place of anger. But none of those choices will change your reality or improve your future. In fact, those choices simply cause you to stack up *more* lost time by using your time in a way that keeps you stuck rather than moving you forward. Making peace with lost time takes:

- **Forgiveness.** Giving yourself the grace to be human and make mistakes is the first step to peace. If you'd known how things would turn out, you would have made a different choice. But you didn't know. Of course, you should have recognized your worth and value, slowed down before making the decision, or had the faith to believe for better. But whatever the reasons, you did not. And now you know the consequences, which also means next time you'll have the wisdom to know better. Will you forgive yourself?

- **Self-compassion.** If your best friend had lost time in circumstances similar to your own, what would you say to her? How would you comfort and encourage her? The idea of self-compassion is to treat yourself the way you'd treat someone you really care about. You would not make your best friend feel worse about it or beat her up for it. So why do that to yourself? Making peace with lost time means having compassion for your own humanity, being gentle with yourself, and acknowledging the hardship you endured.

- **Gratitude.** Giving thanks in the midst of pain shifts your focus from loss to opportunity. Today is the first day of the time you have left. By looking at what remains, you can make a choice about what you want to do with today and the rest of your future. It takes emotional and spiritual maturity to have gratitude when you don't get what you want, and it also gives you the strength to make the most of what you have left.

When I found myself in the unwanted place of having lost time, these profound acts empowered me to have hope. I made the choice to be grateful for the opportunity to start my life over. I decided not to give up on my heart's desire for marriage and family. I looked for the lessons from my experience. I wanted to know life would unfold as I hoped, but there were no guarantees. And sometimes that meant I cried until I had no tears left, and all that remained was my choice to trust that God still had a plan for my life that aligned with the desires I believe were divinely placed in my heart. The other choice was to believe that my desires were impossible and improbable—that my lost time was my only time and my entire future would be spent in regret. I decided I'd rather choose hope, even if it meant I never got what I was hoping for. By choosing hope, I took actions that reflected my vision for the future.

Eventually, my hope manifested in a deep and meaningful relationship with my husband. Even so, my hope for children unfolded in a very different way than I had imagined. With marriage came the blessing of two bonus daughters. Amazingly, their names were names I had written long ago in my journal that I wanted to name my daughters if I had girls.

Though I'll never know if in those lost years I would have been able to conceive and bear children, the amazing truth is it doesn't really matter to me now. I have no regrets and no bitterness. My son was not born in my womb but in my heart. The love and connection we have is beautiful and sweet and precious beyond words. I feel so honored that God saw fit to make me his mom, and in retrospect, I wouldn't want things to have worked out any other way. The children we are raising are the children I was meant to raise. The person I became through the death of my first marriage and the discovery of a deeper understanding of my own faith, courage, and resilience is irreplaceable. I would not trade my lost time for the life I live now.

In my emotional transition from one season of my life to the next, a close friend and mentor shared with me an inspiring scripture I'd never paid much attention to: "I will repay you for the years the locusts have eaten" (Joel 2:25). I felt as though years had been wasted, and yet I resolved not to be bitter. The idea that maybe, just maybe, God would make up for these lost years revived my hope. I held on to this promise. I read it often, especially when I began to doubt.

The reality is that time lost may mean dreams deferred or even denied. But if you are willing to adapt by opening your mind to a variation of your dream, you may find that lost time is an opportunity to begin again, to dream a new dream, and to emerge from the challenge wiser, stronger, and determined to make the most of the time you still have. That means making choices to avoid the heartbreak of lost time in the future.

PREVENTING LOST TIME: EMPATHY FOR YOUR FUTURE SELF

I began this chapter with this thought, and I want us to revisit it to break it down further: *One of the consequences of living in a way that allows false urgencies to drive our decisions is that we hyperfocus on the present without looking up to consider a future created by our present-day choices. This takes reflection. It takes intention. It takes planning.*

- **Reflection.** When making choices about the direction of your life, it is important to pause and reflect on the significance of a given decision in order to establish how meaningful it is to your time. Remember that what is meaningful is timeless. It matters now, and it matters in the future. Picture your future self and the choice your future self will wish you had made. This is, in essence, having empathy for your future self by reflecting on how it will feel if you do not make wise choices in the present.

- **Intention.** Choosing the meaningful is an intentional act. It is not haphazard. It means having a vision for where you are going and how you want to spend your time. Dr. Laura King, a researcher and psychologist at the University of Missouri, has studied the impact of writing in the present tense about your "best possible future self" and found that it yields health benefits and an increased sense of meaning in life. It is also the first step to making a plan of action.[1]
- **Planning.** To plan is to care for your future self. It is facing the reality about the present so you can see clearly what next step to take—or not take. And it takes courage to plan because it requires hope for a future with a specific and desired outcome. Planning is creating a road map for where you want to go in the future and then finding a road and a vehicle to get there.

If we are honest with ourselves, we can admit that we often end up making decisions that are motivated by fear and self-sabotage. For example, when I became brutally honest with myself, I realized that turning thirty influenced the urgency I felt about marriage the first time. I also acknowledged I did not have complete peace about my decision, yet I moved forward with logical rationalization. When it comes to making a decision about marriage, time is your friend. It will reveal all that needs to be revealed. It may take longer for the relationship to develop than you want it to, but you will save yourself the heartbreak and regret of lost time if you are patient and do not allow external expectations to force you to make a decision prematurely.

When we refuse to be honest about the fears that motivate our decisions, and we find ourselves in the murky aftermath of those choices, we cannot reclaim our time in the future. We can only look ahead with self-compassion and forgiveness, admitting our faults and mistakes in an effort to prevent ourselves from repeating them.

LOOKING BACK TEN YEARS FROM NOW, WHAT WILL YOU WISH YOU HAD DONE?

One way to keep ourselves from later regretting how we've chosen to spend our time is to consider the perspective of our future selves. In order to live a life that is meaningful and not simply a life in which we react to the demands of our immediate environment, we must pause to consider the person we will one day be. What would she tell us if she had the chance? Pause for just a moment right now and consider the most pressing challenge or opportunity before you. Consider how you are currently handling it. Then ponder this question: Looking back ten years from now, what will you wish you had done?

You may wish you had acted with patience rather than fear because a hasty move is going to result in lots of wasted time. You may wish you had had more faith and gone for it, whatever "it" is. You may wish you had let go of some of your projects and focused more on quality time in your relationships. You may wish you had dropped the grudge and spent more time forgiving and nurturing relationships and less time being bitter. Somehow, when you close your eyes and imagine your future self, you gain the wisdom of hindsight. A simple shift in perspective can help you avoid the tragedy of lost time.

But here's the thing. The first step to getting unstuck from poor choices is telling yourself the truth. Too often, the truth scares us, and so we pretend all will be well and march forward as though the consequences will not catch up with us.

BEING OVERWHELMED LEADS TO POOR DECISIONS AND LOST TIME

Not all lost time is about major life decisions. Sometimes it is the frustration of having committed to a project, event, or purchase you wish you had not. At the core of most lost-time decisions is the choice to put off the hard work of planning, getting clarity, and counting the costs. It is precisely when you don't have time to lose that you are most likely to make decisions that will ultimately lead to lost time. The busier you are, the more likely you are to put off the deep thinking you need to do.

I've been there. In fact, not too long ago I found myself quite frustrated at my own lack of planning and counting the costs.

I received an impassioned and persuasive request to do an event. After a few weeks, an answer was needed and I was about to go on vacation. I felt pressured to make a decision so I could finish my to-do list and enjoy some downtime. I did not have time to think through the implications and pitfalls or even the necessity of doing the event. Feeling the pressure to a make a decision, enthusiasm on the part of the host, and the relief of crossing the decision off my list, I said yes.

I didn't think much about it again until it was time to prepare. That's when I looked at it with clearer vision and felt certain I should have instead said no. I didn't adhere to my own boundaries because I was drawn into the hype of the opportunity. Optimism kicked in, and I didn't think it through. The cost was more than just my time, but also my team's time, so it took time away from other priorities. The cost of undoing the decision would be too high, since many people were involved—they'd now made commitments based on my decision, and reneging on that would cost them money and strain relationships. The time that was lost was time that could have been spent with my family, resting and rejuvenating at home, or doing anything more meaningful than the event I hastily committed myself to.

Perhaps you have found yourself in similar scenarios. There are several habits that can make it more likely that you'll lose time by not stopping to accurately count the cost. I want to share a little about each so that you can determine if any of these is plaguing you:

- Changing gears
- Goal fatigue and decision fatigue
- The paradox of choice

CHANGING GEARS

Have you ever had the feeling of being too overwhelmed to think straight? The truth is you can give your attention to only a limited number of tasks before your decisions and performance begin to suffer. Changing gears constantly from one focus to the next makes you less and less efficient. And yet, this seems to be the way many of us try to get through our days. We come up with a to-do list filled with far more things that we'll ever be able to humanly accomplish and insist to ourselves that we are being reasonable: "If I just stay focused, I can get through this." And maybe you do on Monday, but if you have to keep up that same pace on Tuesday, and then again on Wednesday, eventually you will crash. You won't have the energy. Your willpower will diminish.

It is not just about not having enough time. It is how packed your time feels because you are pulled in so many directions. Stressful thoughts take up space and clarity, causing you to *feel* as though you have more to do than is actually on your plate.

My biggest struggle in this area has been what I call "changing gears": moving from one unrelated task to another. It takes a while to refocus and settle into something new. And to do so, and then have to stop and accomplish something else and then something else is taxing. I may be able to do it once, but the third or fourth time I'm changing gears I no longer feel able to make great decisions or be as productive. So when you've had a day in which you are constantly changing gears, you are more likely to make a decision you later regret. In fact, when you feel pressed for time, you are more likely to make quick decisions just to get the decision off your plate.

GOAL FATIGUE AND DECISION FATIGUE

Goal fatigue and decision fatigue are real, psychological phenomena that occur because we have only so much energy—and it gets used up as we do things that require our attention. For example, the discipline and self-control required to stay on schedule get worn thin. If you don't take breaks and replenish your energy, you have less self-control the next time you attempt to do the very same task.

Focusing on efficiency is effective only when you give yourself the breathing room to recover from the effort required to exercise the self-control to be efficient. Without that margin, setting the expectation to get more done in less time on a continual basis is self-sabotage.

If you're anything like me, a recovering procrastinator, it would be accurate to say that you work well under pressure. A deadline gets you moving. Accountability makes you take action. Some pressure can be a good thing. The problem arises when pressure becomes the only way you live. When efficiency is the only option, you cannot be at your best. People and things that deserve more of your attention do not get it. How do you know when that's you? One way is to notice how easily you are distracted by easier tasks. It is almost as though your brain is just looking for a way to get some relief, to not be so focused, to have a chance to play.

The intense focus required to be efficient all the time is both unhealthy and unsustainable. While pondering this idea, I ran across some fascinating research about why it can be more difficult to consistently make wise financial decisions when you are on a limited budget or are financially strapped. When each decision you make has higher consequences, you spend much more energy making those decisions. You have to pay a lot more attention at the grocery store because every dollar counts. You worry as it gets closer to payday and your funds are running low. It becomes harder to focus because you are juggling just to make the basics work. "Do I fill up my tank so I can make it to work or buy the items my kids want for lunch tomorrow? Maybe I can find a way to skimp on both and still get by." Basically, your brain gets so exhausted from constantly thinking so hard about every decision that eventually you run out of mental energy to keep it up. However, when money is not an issue, you swing by the gas station on the way home and fill up the tank before making an unplanned stop for takeout at your favorite restaurant. No mental energy expended whatsoever. You can save that energy for big-picture decisions and planning.

The same holds true when you have breathing room in your schedule. Your mental resources are not drained dealing with the basics. However, there is one caveat: while having to be efficient all the time with no breathing room can actually make you less efficient, having an overabundance of time can do the same.

PARADOX OF CHOICE

Another norm that has dramatically changed over the years is the overabundance of choices you have about pretty much anything you want—from the multitude of coffee choices at Starbucks to the number of dating apps and the myriad of people on those apps. Some choice is good, but too much choice is overwhelming and time-consuming, according to researcher Dr. Barry Schwartz, author of *The Paradox of Choice: Why More Is Less*.[2] It's easy not to notice the impact of an overabundance of options on your time and happiness, but it can be debilitating, exhausting, and anxiety-producing. Having too many options can paralyze you when it is time to make a decision because you are simply overwhelmed. As a result, you put off decisions, and when you finally make one, it can leave you less satisfied about the choice you did make. Regret is more likely because you wonder later about the other choices you left on the table.

Here's the thing. Not only is it self-sabotage to have too many options, but having no options is terrible for your well-being because you can feel stuck, hopeless, and even demoralized. The ideal is to have *some* choices, but not so many that you get overwhelmed. If you want to feel happier and save time in today's world, you must deliberately *limit* your choices when making a decision. This is true whether the decision is as trivial as what to order for lunch or as significant as which new car to buy or job to take. When I wrote *Successful Women Think Differently,* I dedicated an entire chapter to the problem and process of overcoming this paradox of choice, but here's the most important part. Take a moment to clarify what is most meaningful to you about a particular decision. Make a list of the minimum standards the decision must meet. For example, if you are deciding whether to say yes to an invitation to attend an event, your minimum standards might include the following:

- You really want to go.
- It's an opportunity to build on important relationships rather than taking time away from them.
- It doesn't interfere with something more meaningful.

Using just those three criteria, you'll be able to make better decisions without wasting time going back and forth about it. If we can limit our choices by clarifying what will make the choice meaningful, then we lessen the chance of regret and second-guessing.

This is especially true for big choices that have consequences for lost time that are significant or even devastating. Let's say you're making a decision about a potential spouse. The process is still the same. Make a list of your minimum standards. For example, your standards could be in the form of PQs you must be able to authentically say yes to in order to move forward:

- Do you feel completely at peace about moving forward with the relationship?
- Do you share the same faith and core values?
- Do you have a shared vision for your future together?
- If your mate never changed, would you be happy with them for the rest of your life?

If the answer to any of these questions is "I'm not sure," "no," or "kind of," then it is a sign that moving forward at this time could mean serious regret and lost time in the future. When the decision is a big one, we are more vulnerable to the feelings of urgency that can cause us to ignore warning signs. *If I don't take this opportunity now, will I ever get the chance again?*

The key to good decisions is being truthful with yourself and then having faith that if it is not meant to be, there is a better option for you on the horizon.

CHOOSING IS A POWERFUL ACT

To choose is to create—a memory, a situation, a relationship, a path forward, or a path backward. Whether you choose well or choose poorly, your choices largely create your future. Because we often don't consider that we are making choices, we can unconsciously commit our time in ways we don't recognize until it's too late. Looking back, it is, of course, obvious. But in the moment, if you do not honor the value and preciousness of your time by pausing to reflect on the consequences of your choices as you make them, regret may be inevitable.

#MEANINGFULOVERURGENT

Every choice that has an impact on your future should be made through the lens of several PQs:

- Will my future self be glad I did this?
- If it turns out this was a poor decision, how much time will I have lost?
- If it turns out to be a poor decision, how will I overcome the consequences?
- Is this a wise choice?
- Am I at peace about this choice?

Perhaps the most painful reality of modern life is lost time. When fears, distractions, and seemingly urgent challenges steal your focus from the meaningful moments and purposes that are calling you, you can find yourself longing for the time you may have squandered.

WHEN THE MEANINGFUL CHOICE IS THRUST UPON YOU

Not every choice is of our own doing. Some choices were never a part of our vision, and yet they hold meaning because they test the very core of who we are. When I was twenty-eight years old and my mother was forty-nine, she had a massive brain aneurysm early one December evening while we were talking on the phone after work. We didn't realize at first just how serious it was when her head suddenly began hurting, but within a few hours I found myself at the emergency room signing paperwork for my mother to be rushed into emergency brain surgery. She remained in a coma for three days and didn't leave the hospital for nearly two months. She had lost her speech, her vision, her ability to swallow, sit up, and walk, and her bladder function.

I was heartbroken over my mother's disabilities. I didn't understand why this happened to her. But that didn't change the fact that it did.

I had made the full-time leap into writing and speaking earlier that year, and I was building my business from scratch. But none of that mattered in comparison to being there for my mom and then-eight-year-old brother. I rented out my condo and moved into her house thirty miles away. I didn't ponder my choices much because there was little time. Because of the medical care I had to give my mom, I couldn't be away from the house for more than three hours at a time.

The choice I made during that season was the choice most of us would make in that situation—the meaningful choice to protect and care for those we love. My mother had the challenges of learning to walk and talk again, of endless appointments with neurologists, ophthalmologists, neuro-ophthalmologists, and urologists as well as speech, physical, and occupational therapists. Sometimes in life we have seasons in which we are called to tend to a situation we wish had never come to be.

Today my mother has recovered most of her physical abilities, and I cannot imagine having made any other choice during that season of our lives. It was the meaningful choice, and a season that changed me for the better—even though I would not have chosen for her to go through what she went through. It was my divine assignment for a period of time, and I feel God gave me the grace and strength to handle the abrupt transition from single twenty-something with no children to primary caregiver for my mom and co-parent for my brother.

Difficult seasons are not forever. The meaningful choice may present unexpected hardships, but it is the timeless choice—the one you will be glad you made.

VALUING YOUR TIME

If you haven't already created your time chart, as explained in the introduction, do that now. The chart helps you see in real numbers just how valuable your time is because it illustrates just how little of it you actually have left after your fixed-time expenses. You may notice categories where you are accumulating lost time. For example, if you are anything like the average person and spend over an hour per day scrolling social media, looking at online stores, or playing online games, you'll see quickly how that time adds up, especially over an entire week or month. Don't beat yourself up. Instead, recognize that having numbers in front of you gives you the information you need to see what you can change. The good news is you've now taken the time to get some clarity. We'll use that clarity in upcoming chapters to help you transform how you choose to spend your time.

· ·

MEANINGFUL MINUTE

Revisit your time chart. Where are you "losing time" with activities or choices that are not meaningful? What would be a more meaningful choice in this season of your life? Are you willing to make that new choice? When?

_____

_____

_____

_____

CHAPTER SEVEN

IF YOU HAD THE TIME . . .

As we cleared the dinner table last night, I felt like we were making good time. You know what I mean by that, right? When you have school-age kids, that period between getting home and going to bed sometimes feels like you're trying to herd cats as you plow through a head-spinning number of sequential tasks—making sure the kids do their homework and have some time to play, dinner gets cooked and served, everybody eats some vegetables, you don't leave the kitchen looking like a tornado tore through the house, and everybody goes to bed clean with a little time for bedtime stories, songs, and prayers. And then once you get through all that, you finally get to take a shower and have some sort of bedtime routine of your own—or you lie across the bed for a minute to catch your breath and end up passing out from exhaustion. It feels like an Olympic event between 7:00 and 9:00 p.m. on weeknights.

Last night we were on track, and I was feeling *good*. Then Alex, my four-year-old son, walked into the kitchen from the direction of the front door, proudly interrupting my focused productivity. He moved toward me deliberately, as if it was his mission to remind me that I was, in fact, *not* on track. He slipped his sweet little hand into mine, oblivious to the plates balancing in my other hand as I walked diligently to the sink.

"Mommy, it's time to go watch the sun set!" he exclaimed matter-of-factly as he began guiding me toward the front door. His demeanor was so sure, like, *This is what we do.* No different from, "It's time to eat dinner" or "It's time to go to school."

It was in that moment that I realized our gravitation to watch the sun's spectacularly colorful goodbye at the end of each day had become a ritual. "What will it do tonight?" had become our collective curiosity after dinner, especially now that spring had arrived.

Partly cloudy days are the best. The colors bounce off the clouds and create irresistible works of art in the evening sky. Last night it was so vivid, it looked electric. As the sun lowered over the tree-filled horizon, rays of gold burst through a canvas of creamy clouds and soft pink sky brushed with streaks of periwinkle, fuchsia, and fluorescent coral.

"It's beautiful tonight, Mommy. Look!" Alex said, reaching for the door handle. And that's when I saw a sight that magnified the beauty of the moment: ten-year-old Addie standing barefoot and still between two columns on the porch, awestruck by the sunset. She didn't move or say a word as we joined her on the porch. She just continued to take it all in, giving her full attention to a magnificent vision that would disappear in a matter of minutes.

Jeff and I had made a big deal about the sunsets we are blessed to watch from our new home. How serendipitous that our enthusiasm was contagious and now the children were beating us to the show. To watch a ten-year-old mindfully savor such divine splendor is inspiring. To have your four-year-old lead you to it is deep joy.

Sunset watching has become a daily manifestation for us of the art of choosing the meaningful over the urgent. The sunset never fails to arrive daily, gently nudging us toward the natural rhythm that is always beating in our lives if we are willing to dance to it. When we set out on this transformation journey, the vision was an extremely practical one: put ourselves in a position to work less so we could have more margin in our lives. Work, after all, takes up quite a bit of time. So with less work, there would be more breathing room, more time to just be. But as we experimented with change and shifts began to unfold, we realized our vision was uninspired. A vision must be more than an absence of something you don't want—in this case, too much work. A vision needs to be an aspiration that reaches for something you want. The absence of something can make space for you to manifest the vision, but the absence of something can never *be* the actual vision. A powerful vision is awe-inspiring. It creates something—a memory, a message, an experience, a legacy.

On our honeymoon, we scribbled our vision on little pages of a resort notepad. We keep those notes in our bedroom and glance at them from time to time to see if we are moving in the direction of the vision we prayed for and talked about during walks on the beach. I revisited those sacred little scraps of paper recently. "Let's create a unique experience and an adventure for our family," one of them said.

As simple of an act as it is, when we gather on the front porch of our unexpected home situated on a little hill that points us west—and we gaze at the sunset until it disappears—we are in the vision. The vision of "a unique experience and an adventure" is broad yet specific. We can make it what we want, but it gives us direction, and when we land somewhere unpredicted but gratifying, it gives us meaning too.

When you embark on a journey to conquer time tyranny, you move from losing time to finding it. And when you find time, your next move is to choose how you will spend it. In the next few chapters, we'll dive into the experiments you can try that will empower you to prevent lost time. But what you choose to do with your newfound time is just as important. The art of choosing the meaningful is the art of creating a life in which you are fully present and able to use your time in ways that make your life more authentic and joyful, purposeful and satisfying. The possibilities for what you can do with your found time are abundant.

I invite you to begin imagining what using your found time well might look like for you. What is it that you'd like to see unfold? Maybe you want to feel relaxed in the evenings, with time to connect in your relationships or to take a bubble bath rather than a speedy shower. Perhaps your vision is a business of your own so your schedule can be more flexible. You could even wake up when the sun wakes you up— no alarm clock. Or perhaps you want to focus more on home during this season of your life. That might mean not working at all, or it could just mean not taking on demanding opportunities during this time. Whatever it is, begin imagining a vivid picture of what it looks like to "find time" in this season of your life.

As a coach, I stretch clients to consider far more options than they currently believe are possible. Many find this uncomfortable. Our natural inclination is to put limits on our possibilities in order to stay safe. In a primitive sense, it is self-preservation. Remaining within the boundaries of what you know feels secure. Outside those boundaries is the uncertainty of the unknown. And even when the vision is something we truly want, uncertainty provokes fear. Fear demands that we shrink: make the dream smaller and life will feel safer. Less change, less fear. But limiting yourself to only what feels comfortable can be self-sabotage. At some point, most things and people in your life were unknown. Your skills, your home, your friends, even your spouse or significant other were all once new. Yet here you are—the boundaries of your life's territory expanded and the fears you once felt are not nearly so strong, if they exist at all.

My life's work is coaching others past fear so they achieve their highest purpose and potential, and yet sometimes I have to coach myself past pangs of doubt that creep into my consciousness. The doubts can be persistent: *Are you sure y'all made the right move? Sunsets are not that big a deal. The dream of flying and an airstrip? Is all that really necessary? And you want to work every other day? Business owners aren't supposed to do that. What do you think makes you any different?* You know the doubts I'm talking about, right? It's the internal spiritual battle that ensues when you decide to walk in your purpose, to defy the status quo and live your life as if this is your one chance to live it. When you begin to envision your possibilities, fear is inevitable, but it is not a stop sign. A meaningful life means saying no even when it is hard and saying yes to what is purposeful for you even when it frightens you.

I invite you to step out of your comfort zone and consider the key markers that might let you know you are on track with choosing the meaningful over the urgent. Think of these markers like guideposts that confirm you are on the right path. The marker could be a simple one, like watching the sunset after dinner. Or it could be something that feels more significant—like living near extended family or close friends. *What is it that your soul longs for?* Take a deep breath, close your eyes, and notice what comes up as you ponder that question.

When we slow down and pay attention, all sorts of thoughts can bubble up. We can get to know ourselves on a much deeper level, which is hard to do when we are racing through life and filling up every potential quiet moment with technology and information. Quiet gives you bandwidth to hear the divine whispers of wisdom that are drowned out by the noise of false urgencies.

DIG BELOW THE SURFACE

Here's the thing: it is easy to blame a lack of time for our issues with time. But often it isn't a lack of time that is the real problem—it's our habits.

When I first laid out my vision at the start of this project, I was sure I just needed more time. It was my work that was the problem. I was doing too much of it. Maybe I needed to cut back. Maybe I should start planning my early retirement so I could have more time. I took some quiet time, and as I always try to do when I need direction, I prayed.

As I settled in and sought wisdom, I had the distinct sense that I was way off base with the idea that a lack of time was my problem. The message that came to me was that I have spent twenty years building something that God is not done with. When I did my own time chart like my husband had done, I learned I really didn't spend nearly as much time working as I—or anyone else—thought. When I was honest with myself, I had to admit to some underlying issues that made me *feel* like I lacked time:

- **Procrastination.** I have jokingly referred to myself as a recovering procrastinator for years now. I have a tendency to push off what I need to do today and find other stuff to do instead. Then I feel rushed and pressed for time as a deadline approaches.
- **Perfectionism.** My procrastination is fueled by perfectionism. I believe perfectionism is rooted in the fear that you won't get it right, so you hesitate to even get started. Perfectionism can also show up when you don't think you or your work measure up, so you do everything you can to make sure there are no flaws.
- **Distractions.** I am easily tempted by the distractions of pretty much anything—laundry, clutter-clearing, long-overdue filing. Distractions that aren't that pressing eat up my time and delay me from having to focus.
- **People-pleasing.** Saying yes to things that need a *no* has too often obligated my time to false urgencies. Optimism has caused

me to believe I could do it all and ushered me into feeling overwhelmed more times than I can count.

- **Extending deadlines.** When the time approaches and I realize
  I won't finish a project in time, extending the deadline means
  the project invades days and hours that were intended for something else.
- **Not asking for help.** Going it alone means multiplying the time
  it takes to do just about anything.

I have often planned and scheduled time for a project, then found
myself doing something else during the time I'd designated. Before I
know it, the time is gone, I've made no progress, and I'm pressed for
time. Looking at this list of unflattering habits, I realized lack of time
was not the problem at all. Neither was work. My long-standing, self-
sabotaging habits were the problem, and I needed to address them.
As I embraced this and began dealing with the real issues, my vision
changed too. My focus became managing myself.

As my vision shifted, so did my key markers. In addition to sunset watching, I have two other key markers that are truly meaningful
for me:

- **Flow.** Flow is the state when you are so engaged in what you are
  doing that time seems to fly by. Whether you are fully engaged
  with a person or a project or an activity, there is an ease and
  satisfaction. The challenge in front of you is a perfect match for
  the skill and passion you bring to the moment. Distractions are
  just background noise.
- **Unburdened free time.** This is free time that is unencumbered
  by the feeling that you should be doing something else because
  there is a looming project or pending deadline. Unburdened free
  time means you are not procrastinating. The time is truly yours,
  unindebted to other commitments.

#MEANINGFULOVERURGENT

How about you? What are two or three key markers that let you know
you are on track with choosing the meaningful over the urgent?

_____

_____

_____

MOVING INTO A NEW SEASON

Sometimes the things that used to work for you simply don't anymore.
The grace to do them has run out. The traffic that didn't bother you
much suddenly stresses you out. The heavy load you've carried with
grace as others looked on in awe suddenly feels crushing and burdensome. The projects that felt energizing have begun to lose your interest.
If we pay attention when this happens rather than ignore the change in
our energy, it can be an invitation to reimagine our vision. Seasons of
life are just that—seasons. They are not meant to go on forever. Unless
we imagine what a new season could look like, we can find ourselves
squandering what could be newfound time.

When you become more intentional about making choices that
prevent you from losing time, the opportunity of found time presents
you with this question: What does meaningful look like in this next
season of your life?

My friend Lisa seems to have mastered the art of noticing when a
season is coming to an end and then reimagining her vision. She did it
when she left her job as a television producer for a major news network
after she and her husband had the first of their three children. They
learned to live on one income, a choice that became more challenging
with each new addition to the family. But they did it. "For us, it wasn't

a financial choice. It was a values choice," she explains. "This was something that was important and meaningful to us," she says, pointing out that they lowered expectations about things like cars, clothes, and dining out. The money just wasn't there for those expenses.

After a few years, an opportunity arose to move to Orlando, Florida, to plant a church there, and over time, the church grew to almost 200 members. Things were really beginning to flow when the recession hit in 2008. As people lost their jobs, they uprooted themselves for work in other states or to be near family. Over the course of eight months, the church lost 80 percent of its families as the congregation dwindled to just twenty members. She says they weren't sure what God was up to, but she and her husband prayed hard about it.

Around that time, Lisa got a call out of the blue from the national television network she'd left after the birth of her daughter ten years earlier. They wanted to know if she'd come back. She quickly turned them down. It would mean a move to another state and a lot less time at home. It would be a complete shift in their vision, and neither she nor her husband had contemplated that idea. Then the network called a second time. "Are you sure?" they probed. She was sure and said no once again. But they were persistent, and when they called a third time, they convinced her to come for a visit and chat about the opportunity.

Lisa talked it over with her husband. The truth was, the season for their church plant seemed to be winding down. Finances were very uncertain. Although they'd not imagined moving back to their previous city or Lisa going back to work yet, maybe it was a divine message. It couldn't hurt to have a conversation. So they made the trip with the whole family in tow.

The network painted a vision for Lisa of just why they wanted her specifically. They knew of her strong faith and work in the church. And they liked and trusted her ability to get the job done. On the particular news show for which she was interviewed, they regularly brought on guests of differing viewpoints, and the guests who brought a religious viewpoint—especially a Christian one—were often extreme and came across as out of touch, a slight bit off-kilter, and judgmental. The host was also a believer and wanted Lisa to bring on guests who portrayed Christianity in a more fair and flattering way that more accurately represented the general public.

She was intrigued. Suddenly, the opportunity had special meaning. She could influence what millions of viewers would see. She would not be going back to the same job she'd had ten years earlier; she'd instead be embarking on a job with a specific and meaningful purpose for her.

"I always felt called to secular media," Lisa says. "I always wanted to be a light, and I felt that was my specific purpose in my career."

If this specially created job opportunity wasn't confirmation enough, while Lisa was being interviewed, her husband received a call from an old boss. His new company was looking for a unique combination of skills: someone with experience as a pastor and experience in sales. He could work from home. If he wanted the job, it was his.

And with that, the two of them packed up their family and moved in under two weeks' time. They stepped into a new vision, just as the last of their three children, then age four, entered school.

For the next two years, their lives looked dramatically different from their life in Florida, when they were a pastor and a stay-at-home mom. Lisa began work in the late morning and could see the kids off to school. Since her husband was now a work-from-home dad, someone was there when the kids got home. Her bosses were supportive of requests for time off for recitals and sick kids. But Lisa rarely arrived home before mid-evening, and soon her husband was promoted and began to travel. They tried hiring nannies to pick up the kids. They juggled responsibilities. They managed their calendars meticulously. But frankly, it was exhausting.

"My husband became head of sales and marketing and had to commute two hours round trip rather than working from home," she recalls. "I wasn't home until seven, and if it was breaking news, there was no telling. If I was working, he cooked. If he was out of town, it was 'tag, you're it.' It was becoming a lot of chaos. Our parents live in another state. My sister lives in Florida and my husband has no siblings. For us, our core value was that we grow closer to God and each other. Instead, we realized if we weren't careful we would be living two separate lives. Our kids were disengaging from us at a time when my oldest was dealing with middle school and mean girls. I was learning to deal with a traveling husband and two full-time careers, but we just weren't feeling it. The larger income didn't outweigh the benefits of being present with each other and our kids."

The vision that worked for them a couple of years earlier was becoming a bad dream. But there was one ray of light. When Lisa worked, she had always earned more than her husband. Now, for the first time in their marriage, her husband's income exceeded hers. This gave them more security than they'd had before. Sensing another moment of choice, they prayed and listened for guidance. They reimagined their lives once again.

"I remember going in and telling the incredible group of women I worked with that I would be leaving and going home," she says. "I cried as I told them, in part because I realized how good I had it as a woman in a place of influence working in a supportive environment."

She was surprised by their reaction, though. Not only did her bosses tell her the door to her job would remain open, but they truly connected with her decision. Like Lisa, these women were in their thirties and forties, in the prime of their careers, doing the work they'd once hoped to have the chance to do. "Every one of them said if they could afford to do what I was doing, they would do it." She was perplexed. "It was supposed to be our time. Our kids were all in school. Why would we go back home again?" In other words, these women had what they wanted, but they wanted more time for the meaningful.

Sitting over lunch with Lisa several years ago, I could feel the purpose and energy of her decision so much that it has resonated with me ever since. She is a woman who, again and again, has chosen the meaningful by being sensitive to the power of grace to give her strength to carry out a vision. When grace left, she asked, "What is my soul longing for? What does my family long for in this season? What direction do we feel at peace about moving toward?" With those questions, she remained open and flexible to a fluid and inspired vision. When I asked her to describe today what that choice has meant for her and her family, she painted a vibrant picture of a meaningful life.

WHAT'S YOUR AWE-INSPIRING VISION?

Your story is different, but in her story, we see the power of an inspired vision. We see the way a journey can unfold unexpectedly when we are willing to let go so we can find the courage to step out of an old season and into a new one. Sometimes it's big moves like new jobs, new cities, and new schooling. And sometimes it's small moves that feel like major milestones.

Remember Marie, the single mom who tried to go to a meeting and her father's heart surgery in the same morning, but ended up getting to the hospital too late to see him before the surgery? The heartbreak of missing what turned out to be her last chance to see him alive became a turning point in her life. A new vision of what she wanted her life to look like emerged.

When she told her boss about the death of her father and how she'd attended a meeting that morning instead of going to the hospital first thing, her boss was horrified. He actually lived the life Marie was now aspiring to. He always put his family first, and yet he'd advanced quite well in the company. His sense of balance actually made him happier and more productive, he said. It turned out the pressure Marie felt was self-imposed.

Her new and inspired vision centered around a very simple rule: family comes first. Now, pretty much everyone says this, but not everyone lives it. And for Marie, family meant not just her children and relatives, but friends who were like family too.

Many of her close childhood friends who lived in the same city attended her father's funeral. She had often received social invitations from them but never accepted. That changed. Many of these friends were women she loved and enjoyed spending time with but had not seen in more than a year. So she decided she'd get together with old friends at least once a month.

Her previous attitude was "work first." She had convinced herself it was a necessary mantra as a single parent who did not want her children to be deprived of opportunities because of a lack of money. But she dropped that belief and exchanged it for two new ones: (1) quality time was more important than material advantages, and (2) she could still be excellent at work without sacrificing time with her kids. The latter was the most significant. It meant that she would need to be more intentional with her time, and she'd have to work around her children's school schedules and activities. But her vision was this: never miss a game or a recital, volunteer occasionally at their school, and host family dinners for her extended family.

A few years later, Marie's mom was given a very short time to live after being diagnosed with Lou Gehrig's disease. Marie dropped everything to return to the city where she grew up. She fed her mom. She gave her sponge baths. She rubbed her head and showered her with love and kisses and words of encouragement. And when her mom passed, she knew she had made the timeless choice. The guilt she'd felt when her father passed was replaced with the peace of knowing she'd served her mother with great love in her final days.

Your soul may long to find more time without making major changes at work or home. If this season of life calls for you to put more energy into your work, your questions become, "What are my key markers for maintaining a strong connection with the people I care about? What are the key markers that let me know I am making timeless choices and living a vision that is meaningful even years from now?"

My client Victoria has achieved a level of success most in her field will never achieve. She loves her work, and she's excellent at it. She admittedly has never wanted to be a stay-at-home mom. It is simply not her calling. She loves her family and has strong relationships with her children. One of the reasons is that she has created an awe-inspiring vision for her time with them.

"I make my time with my kids memorable. That's my goal," she explains. "I spend a lot of time thinking about creating memories for them. So although I travel a lot, I don't waste the time we have together."

The same energy she puts into her work, she puts into planning time with her kids and husband. "I knew if I was going to pursue a career at this level, I would also need to nurture my family at a level that requires focused attention. I had to make the most of the time we had, or it would be unbalanced, and that can cause problems. I have seen it for others, and I did not want that for my own family."

Now that her children are young adults, the result of her intentionality is that they have always felt valued because of the way their mother made time for them and made it special. And they have a level of confidence and belief in their own possibilities that stems, in part, from watching their mother successfully pursue her dreams. It is a balance Victoria admits has not always been easy. It takes work and intention, but it's well worth it.

In a coaching session in which I probed about how she spent her free time, Leigh, another client, reluctantly admitted that she was too tied to her gadgets. Her online life represented a large chunk of lost time—three or more hours per night on social media, mindlessly scrolling and surfing from one article and post to the next as she lay on the sofa watching television. She'd had a bad breakup a year earlier, and two of her good friends had gotten married, so they didn't spend nearly as much time talking and hanging out as they used to. Rather than imagining a vision for this new season of life that could inspire her, she retreated to nights spent in an online world that seemed to connect her with others but in fact left her quite lonely.

"I tell myself I'll just log on for a few minutes, and before I know it, a couple of hours have passed and it's time to get ready for bed," she said. "It is a hollow feeling, like my time just got swallowed up by a black hole, with nothing to show for it."

"What could you do with your time that would make you feel fulfilled rather than hollow? What would leave you feeling inspired and energized?" I asked.

Leigh let out a light and airy sigh, as if relieved by the very idea that she could feel energized. It was a shift that emerged through a simple but powerful question. She paused to ponder and then began sharing some ideas.

"I would love to spend some time once a week doing something that makes a difference for kids in need," she began. "If I could volunteer even an hour a week, I would feel like I was using my time well. I also want to be around people more. I know two of my friends are focused on their new marriages, but there are other friends I could reach out to but haven't. I'd like to do fun things on weekends or even during the week, but I guess I need to make the effort rather than waiting on people to call me. And I've been talking forever about taking this dance class one of my coworkers told me about. I need to just do it."

In a matter of minutes, Leigh began painting a picture of what she could do with newfound time if she traded the black hole of social media surfing for an intentional and meaningful plan for her time.

In both Leigh's and Victoria's lives, the key was asking what an inspiring vision would look like and giving up time habits that are counter to living in that vision. In order to move toward the meaningful, we must clarify what is not as meaningful and be willing to give it up.

AN INSPIRED VISION GROWS

In Lisa's case, giving up her television job a second time meant down-sizing their lifestyle once again and giving up their home in the center of the city. To go back to one income for a family of five, they moved to the outer suburbs. They found a foreclosure and renovated it. This meant a third house in just a few short years for the kids. So they added an unexpected choice to the already fluid vision: homeschooling.

"In the process of enrolling the kids in school, I met a woman who homeschooled, and she wasn't strange," Lisa recalls jestingly. "I don't mean to be insulting. Obviously we homeschool now, so the same could be said of us, but this family was happy, healthy, and imperfect. Their kids were social. I thought, *Maybe I could do that for a year or two and help my kids stabilize.*" In other words, even after making the leap out of her job, Lisa was still flexible and open to further reimagining the vision. What would be the best use of her newfound time in light of her and her family's needs and values?

They decided to homeschool on a year-by-year basis, an exper-iment of sorts. And the kids "re-up" each year if they want. "The meaningful choice for us was to spend this time being the biggest voice in their lives. There is so much going on in today's culture. We wanted to be the first voice to shape their character and how they process things."

Of the decision, she reflects, "It has been really hard at times. And it has been fantastic. Choosing to spend my time in this way has given me a love for my children I never had. Having more time with them, we grew together. I love hanging out with them." But she was also intentional about creating time for her other relationships, something that had become nearly impossible with the chaotic schedule she'd had. "I have a girls' night out once a week. My husband and I date each other. We are closer as a family."

When her daughter graduated from an online high school recently,

Lisa and her husband sat misty-eyed as she walked the stage to receive her diploma with multiple honors. Her husband said, "It seems like we blinked and she's off to college."

Lisa paused, then joyfully disagreed. "Honey, we didn't blink. Our eyes were wide open the whole time."

Isn't that what we all want—to spend our time in ways that are meaningful with our eyes wide open to the experience, savoring the moments that come only once and creating memories we'll want to revisit for a lifetime?

Major transformation in how we spend our time begins when we notice what's not working and are open to shifting our lives to respond to our needs and the needs of those we love. It continues when we are willing to reimagine the possibilities. When the way we spend our time feels chaotic and burdensome, it is a sign. Your job is to pay attention. You don't have to have all the answers right now, but if you get quiet and listen, they'll start to come to you. Fear will likely accompany them; expect it, but keep imagining. Change is possible.

This quieting of your spirit is not a one-time event. The goal is to make it a way of life. When you do, your path unfolds over time with clear purpose and direction. There are steps you will not see until you've progressed a bit, and you might not feel prepared for what comes next, but over time, as you approach new milestones, you'll become ready. It's like making a turn and suddenly seeing a new landscape that had been blocked from view. New meaningful markers appear and deepen your understanding about what to do with your newfound time.

To get clarity, take a moment to pause and ponder these questions:

What is meaningful for you in this season of your life?

_____

_____

What used to be meaningful that isn't anymore?

_____

_____

Is there a new season calling to you? If so, what does it look like?

_____

_____

What is the vision for your life that you'd like to begin moving toward?

_____

_____

What fears threaten to keep you from embracing a new season or vision?

_____

_____

Your vision is exciting, but inevitably, the journey to achieving it is full of obstacles. But there is hope for blasting through the obstacles. If it took only vision to take charge of your time, your happiness would not be endangered by time tyranny. You'd just write the vision and walk toward it. The most common obstacles are the fears and vulnerabilities that whisper constantly, causing doubt and prompting behaviors that are counterproductive to the vision. Do not allow this to discourage you.

In the next few chapters, I'll equip you with the tools to raise your awareness of the invisible influencers that threaten to throw you off course. It is possible to live timelessly in a world full of false urgencies, but the only people who succeed are those who take charge of their thoughts and conquer the most insidious forces of technology, expectations, and fears that hold most others back.

You are capable of getting to your vision. Let's talk about the knowledge to navigate the obstacles to get there.

- -

MEANINGFUL MINUTE

Spending time getting clarity about your vision is one of the most rewarding investments you will ever make. Even more powerful is identifying key markers that tell you that you are on track and living your vision.

What are three key markers of your vision that you want to remember as you move forward?

_____

_____

_____

Keep these markers in a place where you'll see them daily—in your closet, on the bathroom mirror, or as a screen saver, for example.

CHAPTER EIGHT

THE POWER OF A POSITIVE PESSIMIST

A while back I posted this lighthearted question on social media after what I had thought would be a fifteen-minute errand turned into an hour-and-a-half journey through a maze of tempting detours and hundreds of unhurried weekend shoppers:

"Why did I think I could 'run into Ikea right quick' on a Saturday morning?"

A friend who studied applied positive psychology with me in graduate school at the University of Pennsylvania replied with a one-sentence comment that stopped me in my tracks. It explained in the simplest, most undeniable way my recurring problem of underestimating how much time I need to get anything done:

"Because you are an optimist."

I stared at the screen in astonishment. Scott's five-word observation was a lightbulb moment for me. As ridiculous as it sounds, I believed I could run into a 360,000-square-foot store, quickly locate the item I needed, and breeze through the checkout line in fifteen minutes flat.

One of my greatest strengths—optimism—is a weakness when it comes to estimating time. And I knew it wasn't just this one instance.

Suddenly I had flashbacks to all those times I was late but deep down believed I had enough time to be early. I thought of all the times I set goals at the beginning of the year and honestly thought if I just worked diligently enough, they'd all be accomplished by spring. When I started my business years ago, I wrote a plan that included having my calendar booked solid with speaking engagements within six months. I was so far off. It was about seven years before I was booked the way I had predicted.

ARE YOU AN OPTIMIST?

Optimism is defined as a mental attitude reflecting a belief or hope that the outcome of some specific endeavor, or outcomes in general, will be positive, favorable, and desirable. Optimism, not rudeness, is the reason so many people are consistently late to every appointment. Optimism, not disorganization, is the reason many managers overwhelm their teams with unrealistic expectations and deadlines. Time debt is often caused by time optimism.

Talk of goals and vision and a fresh start inspires you if you're an optimist. Optimists are great goal setters. We are often called "visionaries" for our ability to see great possibilities for the future. Research shows that optimism, in fact, is a predictor of success. It makes sense. When you believe in the possibility of something better, you are more likely to move toward it than people who believe nothing hard is worth trying because they'll probably fail anyway.

And there's one more benefit to optimism in today's world: people like optimists. Optimists are lauded as leaders. They are upbeat and encouraging. They inspire you to keep going. Without optimism, there is no hope. Without hope, there is no dreaming, no goal setting, no starting place for your vision. Without hope, there is no need for faith. Faith, after all, is the substance of things hoped for.

So optimism is necessary for fulfillment, success, and happiness. Being able to see and appreciate the good and believe in possibility is healthy. In fact, my guess is that you have quite a bit of optimism yourself. After all, you have chosen to read a book about how to create a better future.

Research repeatedly confirms many benefits to optimism. Optimists report fewer illnesses and have longer lives, get more promotions and raises at work, and have more friendships. The positive emotion produced by optimism is good for both your mind and body. It boosts your immune system. It strengthens the bonds of your relationships and causes feelings of closeness, which in turn makes it easier to discuss negative events and subjects. It inspires and moves you to action.[1]

But what if your hopes are chronically stressing you out? What if your expectations leave you feeling extra pressure to do things quickly and do too much in too little time? Just because something might be humanly possible doesn't mean it ought to make your to-do list with an expectation of being checked off in record time. A little stress can be good; having no pressure whatsoever can lead to complacency. But excessive pressure is unhealthy. It steals the joy from your journey. It causes you to miss the moments that matter as you race toward the next thing. And sometimes it creates problems you would not have faced had you simply slowed down.

In today's world, where what's normal isn't always natural, a growing list of modern demands can tempt optimists to behave in ways that defy logic. The single parent (or married parent with a traveling spouse) wants to believe she can manage the household, work, and balance multiple activities for her children, and so she packs the schedule optimistically. The professional who travels every week wants to believe that the hectic pace won't negatively impact her personal life, but that expectation is often met with frustration and disappointment.

And the parents with kids who now also find themselves caring for aging parents may find their optimism at being able to maintain their current lifestyle and pace bumps up against the reality of their children's and parents' needs.

Optimism is a powerful character strength. But like any strength, when overused, it can become a weakness. As counterintuitive as it may sound, a dose of strategic pessimism is a necessary skill for getting out of time debt and reversing the norms that can overwhelm and exhaust you.

TIDSOPTIMISM: THE TIME OPTIMIST

Turns out, there is a word for what I did at Ikea that Saturday morning. Apparently I am not alone in this habit of acting on an unrealistic estimate of how much time you need to accomplish something. *Tidsoptimism* is a word that is Swedish in origin, and the literal translation is "time optimism." It describes the person who thinks they have more time than they do, and as a result, is habitually late, running out of time, and trying to catch up.

Hmm . . . Guilty as charged.

When you say yes to a commitment without accurately counting the cost, you are essentially postponing the time it takes to plan. Rather than having empathy for your future self, you are loading up your future self with obligations.

If you are not accurate about the time it will take to complete tasks, you will find yourself making commitments you do not actually have the time to fulfill. And when the commitments arrive, you become stressed at the realization you are once again in time debt. You've lost time because you miscalculated time.

What are some of the ways your propensity for positivity and optimism may be sabotaging how you schedule your life and work?

- Perhaps it is the scheduling of your children's extracurricular activities. You want to give them great opportunities, but you're stressed out trying to keep up with it all. There's no room for spontaneity because your nights and weekends are filled up for months at a time.

- Perhaps you've convinced yourself you can take on multiple projects and still have some sense of balance in your life. Then you beat yourself up for being exhausted. You have the expectation that somehow if you just squeeze in a little self-care, all will be well. You treat a bubble bath like a stop at the gas station to refill your tank, and end up disappointed when your stress returns shortly after emerging from your bubbles to the reality of responsibilities that didn't magically disappear when the water swirled down the drain.

- Maybe you say yes when the best answer would be no. And it might just be your discomfort with disappointing others that fuels your optimism that you can take on more than you actually can.

And what about the big decisions in your life? Optimism, especially when coupled with emotions such as fear or insecurity, can drive you to make major life decisions much too quickly. "Why did I think I could change someone who doesn't want to change?" you're left wondering. "Why didn't I give myself more time to get to know them? To consider my options?" you lament. But by the time you are asking such questions, you've already racked up lost time—sometimes years of it.

TIME TYRANNY THRIVES ON OPTIMISM

Both optimism and pessimism are feelings about the future. Optimism is thinking about the future and asking, "What could go right? What is the opportunity?" Pessimism, on the other hand, is thinking about the future and asking, "What could go wrong? What's the danger? Where am I at risk?" When thinking about time, both sets of questions are important. If you find yourself only focused on risks and danger and what might go wrong, you'll never be motivated to do anything worthwhile with your time. If you find yourself only focused on what's right, what's good, and what's possible, you risk putting yourself in danger of making choices that deplete your time. Optimism will give you the foresight and fortitude to change your relationship with time and create a vision for your future that excites you. Pessimism will give you the ability to prepare for the inevitable obstacles that try to keep you from reaching that vision.

While the foundation of optimism is positive thinking, to have a healthy relationship with time, we must move beyond simple positive thinking to *accurate* thinking, which is optimism rooted in truth. The first step to getting unstuck is always telling yourself the truth, acknowledging reality, and making a plan that accounts for that reality. That means slowing down when making a decision about how you spend your time, whether it is a simple task like running an errand in Ikea, a bigger task such as deciding whether to take on a new commitment, or a life-changing decision such as going back to school or moving to a new city away from family.

The time tyranny that drives us to do too much in too little time insists that if we just try a little harder, we can do more. And "more" always seems to be the goal. Under time tyranny, though, we are always pressed for time, and these are the moments when we are precisely vulnerable to time optimism. It's easy to skim past the details or deny their importance. Then we can optimistically insist that our plan to move forward will succeed, that we have enough time to pull it off. Optimism becomes a crutch that excuses our lack of time, and therefore, lack of thoughtfulness in taking on tasks and activities we never had time to take on in the first place. It feels faster to say yes in the moment than to stop and count the cost. But once we say yes, our future selves are on the hook and more time debt is incurred.

Because optimism tends to produce positive emotion, it is naturally seen as more desirable. We collectively view pessimism as negativity, and therefore, something to be fixed. Some believe this is because pessimism is linked to depression and there is, unfortunately, a stigma around depression. This interpretation is too simplistic, though. The truth is, there are types of pessimism—and while two of the types can be destructive, the third type is constructive and essential to your efforts to break out of time poverty and experience freedom from time tyranny.

THE BEST OPTIMISTS HAVE A PESSIMISTIC STREAK

The first two types of pessimism are *dispositional pessimism* and *explanatory pessimism*.

Dispositional pessimism is the type we typically think of as pessimism. This is the person who, no matter the situation, says it cannot be done. Dispositional pessimists have a generally negative outlook on just about anything. You give them your goal and timeline and their attitude is, "Why even bother because it's not likely to happen anyway?" They'll talk you out of your idea and shake their heads that you are so naive as to have had the idea in the first place. After all, haven't you seen all the people who tried and failed?

Explanatory pessimism is very personal.[2] It is revealed in the way a person explains bad events by attributing the failure to personal shortcomings rather than external forces. So explanatory pessimists have an overloaded schedule because they "just aren't good at saying no." To them, their problem is fixed and unchangeable, thereby dooming them to their circumstances now and forever.

The third type of pessimism, though, is actually a necessary and strategic tool for climbing out of time poverty. It is *defensive pessimism*, a term coined by psychologist Dr. Nancy Cantor.[3] Defensive pessimism looks down the road to see potential problems and proactively takes steps to eliminate or minimize those problems. It is proactive, empowering you to take actions to prevent or reduce the impact of negative outcomes.

Whereas a dispositional pessimist might avoid dating altogether for fear of wasting time and still ending up single, a defensive pessimist would seek out strategies for finding and maintaining a strong relationship and refuse to entertain relationships with those who do not possess the character traits required for a strong, sustained partnership. While a dispositional pessimist might insist on far more time than is needed to accomplish a task and frustrate those who have to work with her, a defensive pessimist carefully plans, calculating the time needed to complete the task as well as the buffer needed for any unforeseen problems or obstacles.

The time optimist, on the other hand, has an aggressive timeline that discounts the time needed for planning, makes no provision for errors, and estimates the time needed to complete the task in a way that can only be pulled off if everything goes perfectly.

The most effective people when it comes to time, those who are "time affluent" instead of time poor, are what I call "positive pessimists." They are dispositional optimists, explanatory optimists, and defensive pessimists. In other words, they have a positive outlook about their possibilities, they don't internalize mistakes and failures, and they are accurate thinkers when it comes to seeing potential problems. They believe in their ability to come up with a plan of action to work around the problem, find people who can help them overcome the problem, or come up with an alternative plan. And their explanatory optimism assures them that they have what it takes to make the necessary changes to succeed. Here's a breakdown of these traits to help you.

DISPOSITIONAL OPTIMISM	DISPOSITIONAL PESSIMISM
• Positive person with a can-do attitude • Always sees the good • Tendency to inspire others • Believes the best about people and situations	• Chronic tendency toward negative emotions • Generally negative outlook on all things • Exhausting and discouraging to others • Believes no amount of forethought will change an outcome
EXPLANATORY OPTIMISM	EXPLANATORY PESSIMISM
• Attributes failure to external forces or temporary shortcomings	• Personalizes failure • Believes their flaws are permanent and will eternally doom them • Attributes positive outcomes to luck
DEFENSIVE OPTIMISM	DEFENSIVE PESSIMISM
• Tends not to calculate the "costs" of a commitment, which can create unreasonable expectations • Overly optimistic attitude, which leads them to overschedule, set tight deadlines, and deny potential time crunches • No margin for error	• Lowers their expectations in preparation for the worst possible outcome • Not generally negative, only in the context of certain goals • Uses anxiety as a preparation tool but is not hindered by it

Note: A positive pessimist possesses three of the above traits—dispositional optimism, explanatory optimism, and defensive pessimism.

ARE YOU A POSITIVE
PESSIMIST? TAKE THE TEST

Positive Pessimism Assessment Questions

In each of the three categories that follow, be as honest as possible and circle the *three* statements that most accurately reflect how you feel *today*. If you struggle to see yourself accurately, ask yourself, "How would the people who know me best answer this question?"

Category 1: Of the following eight statements, circle the *three* statements that most resonate with your beliefs and your life right now and in your recent past. Do not circle the statements you *want* to be true, but the statements that actually *are* true.

1. People often ask me what I'm smiling about and I don't even realize I'm smiling.
2. You have to watch your back at all times because you really can't trust people.
3. I believe most people are inherently good.
4. I don't feel a sense of purpose in my everyday life.
5. People often tell me I inspire them.
6. I sometimes feel that there's not much I can do to change my situation.
7. When things go wrong, I always believe there is a lesson in the situation.
8. Although I'd like to feel differently, it seems my best days are probably behind me rather than in front of me.

Category 2: Of the following eight statements, circle the *three* statements that most resonate with your beliefs and your life right now and in your recent past. Do not circle the statements you *want* to be true, but the statements that actually *are* true.

1. I attribute most of my successes to my
   willingness to work hard and persevere.
2. When I make mistakes, it is typically
   because I tend to get overwhelmed.
3. I am confident that I can change my time habits because
   I have changed other habits in my life in the past.
4. I attribute most of my successes to the lucky
   breaks I've gotten along the way.
5. When I look back at my biggest failure,
   I also see my biggest lessons.
6. When I think about trying to change my time
   habits, I get discouraged because I think
   maybe I'm just stuck in my ways.
7. When I make a mistake, it is typically because
   I did not slow down and pay attention.
8. When I look back at my biggest failure, I realize I'm afraid
   of repeating the same mistake again in the future.

Category 3: Of the following eight statements, circle the *three* statements that most resonate with your beliefs and your life right now and in your recent past. Do not circle the statements you *want* to be true, but the statements that actually *are* true.

1. When estimating how much time something will take, I
   always leave breathing room to finish ahead of schedule.
2. I do my best work under pressure.
3. I tend to get started early on projects so I can take my time.
4. In the last week, I have been late, rushed, or
   missed a deadline because I ran out of time.
5. My default responses to new commitments are,
   "No" or "Let me think about it." I don't say yes
   unless I know for sure I have time to do it.

6. It seems like I'm late about the same amount of time everywhere I go.
7. In the last week, I have been on time everywhere I went, met my deadlines, and had a little time to spare.
8. I often say yes before I think through whether yes is the best answer.

Category 1

Dispositional Optimism: Answers 1, 3, 5, 7
Dispositional Pessimism: Answers 2, 4, 6, 8

Out of the three statements you circled as sounding most like you, in which category did the majority of your answers fall?

_____

If all of your answers fall under the category of dispositional optimism, you exercise that trait often. If two of your three answers fall under dispositional optimism, you lean toward that trait. If none of your answers fall under dispositional optimism, you exercise dispositional pessimism more often than not. Being aware of this fact can help you be more intentional about your outlook on life in general, and your ability to change your time habits in particular.

Category 2

Explanatory Optimism: Answers 1, 3, 5, 7
Explanatory Pessimism: Answers 2, 4, 6, 8

Out of the three statements you circled as sounding most like you, in which category did the majority of your answers fall?

_____

If all of your answers fall under the category of explanatory optimism, you exercise that trait often. If two of your three answers fall under explanatory optimism, you lean toward that trait. If none of your answers fall under explanatory optimism, you exercise explanatory pessimism more often than not. Being aware of this fact can help you be more intentional about your outlook on life in general, and your ability to change your time habits in particular.

Category 3

Defensive Pessimism: Answers 1, 3, 5, 7
Time Optimism: Answers 2, 4, 6, 8

Out of the three statements you circled as sounding most like you, in which category did the majority of your answers fall?

_____

If all of your answers fall under the category of defensive pessimism, you exercise that trait often. If two of your three answers fall under defensive pessimism, you lean toward that trait. If none of your answers fall under defensive pessimism, you exercise time optimism more often than not. Being aware of this fact can help you be more intentional about being realistic when estimating how much time things will take. This can help alleviate unnecessary stress, lateness, missed deadlines, and rushed experiences.

To recap, positive pessimists are:

- Dispositional optimists
- Explanatory optimists
- Defensive pessimists

Use this informal assessment to gauge where you currently stand and determine if you need to work toward developing the key traits to positive pessimism.

POSITIVE PESSIMISM IN ACTION

What if, instead of racing off to Ikea that Saturday morning, I had practiced positive pessimism? I would have paused to add up the time realistically. Thirty minutes to get there would have been a reasonable assessment, although it wasn't a long drive. Accounting for traffic and the parking garage would lengthen my time estimate. I would have recalled my previous visits to Ikea, none of which were less than ninety minutes. It is difficult to get through the store without being lured toward items that are not on my shopping list, so I would have given myself at least ten minutes to get lost.

With just these few pieces of information, I would have decided that this particular day, when I had to be somewhere by late morning, was not a good time to attempt this mission. It was something I wanted to get off of my to-do list, but it wasn't necessary that day. In retrospect, I could have spent less time than it took to drive to Ikea ordering the item online to be delivered to my house.

Looking at the situation now, the answers seem obvious. But that's usually the case. When you are optimistic in the moment, you don't question the urgency. So when "urgency" demands, "Do it now!" you act. You subconsciously buy into the lie that you don't have time to pause and think—and that is the opposite of what you should do. When you feel pressed to react to something that feels urgent, you must train yourself to stop and think. It is a form of mindfulness, which we'll discuss further in a moment. For now, consider these warning signs that can lead you to feel a sense of urgency in decision making:

- Your breathing feels shallow.
- Your body feels tense.
- You feel pressure to hurry up—from yourself and others.
- You feel an obligation financially, circumstantially, or due to a desire not to disappoint.

Whenever these warning signs appear, make it a point to pause. Then follow these steps:

- Breathe. Slowing your breathing calms your thoughts and gives you an opportunity to intentionally choose your course of action.
- Ask, "Is this meaningful or is it a false urgency?" This is a simple but profound question. In most scenarios, you'll have a gut reaction because it is obvious what's meaningful and what's not.
- Ponder, "What am I afraid will happen if I do not succumb to the pressure I feel?" Fear is what most often keeps us from doing what we already know we should. Whether it is fear of rejection, fear of what others might think, or fear of missing out, remember that choosing the meaningful requires courage.
- Choose the meaningful over the urgent. Simple as that. Make a choice.

You may be tempted toward time optimism when you are under pressure because defensive pessimism leads you to admit that you can't do everything on your plate—and you may not know what to do about that. You might be reluctant to change your plans, or to disappoint others or yourself because you can't do all the things you'd like to. So it is easier to insist it is all possible. But this state of optimism sabotages your time and leaves you feeling hurried and frazzled.

You can conquer time optimism by practicing the power of a pause to ask yourself a few simple questions about the urgency and meaningfulness of the task at hand. Just a few minutes of thoughtfulness can empower you to see what you are already wise enough to see if you slow down and refuse to let the pressure of time tyranny rule. Consider a decision you need to make about how to spend your time and ask these questions:

- How will it affect other decisions and goals I've committed to?
- What other things must fall into place in order for it to unfold in a way that has a positive impact on me and not a negative one?
- What are the risks I am taking by saying yes to the goal or decision?
- What risks will I avoid by saying no?

DEFENSIVE PESSIMISM PREVENTS LOST TIME

But it isn't just essential to practice defensive pessimism when it comes to choosing what to put on your schedule. Defensive pessimism is especially useful when you are making major decisions that potentially lead to lost time. Particularly for those who are go-getters, optimism increases over time as your confidence in your ability to accomplish goals increases.

Sometimes the more you accomplish, the more optimistic you are, even when it is not warranted. An extreme example of this is something

Dr. Susan Weitzman calls "upscale abuse." She works with women who have at least a bachelor's degree and often graduate, law, and other advanced degrees—and whose household incomes are more than $100,000—and she found these women often stay in physically abusive marriages longer because they are used to being able to effect change. They have optimism that they can figure it out. "If I just change this, if I just say that, if I just . . ." Believing they control more than they do, they stay and keep making adjustments in hopes things will get better in the future, but the clock keeps ticking and things never change.

So often we are just doing our best to create the lives we've hoped for. And sometimes our ideals are greater than our capacity to achieve them. When this is the case, defensive pessimism is the strategy that can jolt us into reality and empower us to come up with a plan of action that will allow us to break free of time tyranny.

MEANINGFUL MINUTE

When are you most tempted to be a time optimist?

_____

_____

In a situation or project in which you are being a time optimist right now, what would it look like to practice defensive pessimism?

_____

_____

#MEANINGFULOVERURGENT

CHAPTER NINE

BEAUTY IS THE BEAST

I f I talked to the people who know you best and asked them about your most endearing traits, I bet they could tell me some things about you that are truly admirable. Perhaps they'd describe how thoughtful and considerate you are of others. They might mention the way you inspire them with your sense of hope and optimism, even in the face of great odds. Or perhaps it would be your commitment to doing things with excellence. "She likes things done right," they'd tell me, "and she's willing to put in the effort." There are some wonderful innate traits that make you *you*. And I'd love to dwell there. But there's a problem I need you to see. There is a flip side to those wonderful traits: when we overuse them, they can become weaknesses. In other words, what makes you great also makes you vulnerable. I call them Core Vulnerabilities—a response to stress in which we overuse our strengths, creating blind spots that keep us from making wise decisions.

The beauty of your natural strengths can become the beast you must tame. This is especially true when we try to make better decisions with our time. The art of choosing the meaningful requires us to be aware of the vulnerabilities that can steer us in the wrong direction. The same optimism that leads you to set a big goal can also make you underestimate just how much effort it will take and leave you with deadlines you can't possibly meet. Your tendency to be concerned with others' feelings can manifest itself as thoughtfulness on the one hand, and a fear of disapproval that makes it hard for you to say no to time-consuming requests on the other hand. And your noble desire to be fair and do what's right can open the door to guilt trips by those who will twist the narrative in order to get you to spend your time doing what they want no matter what. The list goes on. Let's take a look at these six Core Vulnerabilities, and then I'll help you pinpoint your own Core Vulnerabilities and how to overcome them.

SIX CORE VULNERABILITIES: WHEN STRENGTHS BECOME WEAKNESSES

There are six Core Vulnerabilities:

- Tidsoptimism
- Perfectionism
- Overachieving
- Over-responsibility
- Approval addiction
- Misplaced guilt

When it comes to making meaningful choices with your time, it is essential to become aware of how these vulnerabilities influence your choices. In a few pages, you'll be able to take an assessment to see where you stand on each of these, but let's take a look at the description of each, why they make us more vulnerable to time tyranny, what natural strength they tap into (Beauty), and how they look when that strength is overused (Beast).

TIDSOPTIMISM

Beauty: Hope and optimism are your strengths. You are more willing than most to step out on faith. You always believe you can find a way to get things done.

Beast: As we've already discussed, time optimism, or *tidsoptimism*, is the tendency to underestimate how long things take, which can cause you to take on tasks, deadlines, and goals without an accurate picture of what will be required. It creates unnecessary stress and false urgencies.

PERFECTIONISM

Beauty: You value excellence and a job well done. You are willing to work hard to do things right, and you pay attention to the details that make the difference between average and outstanding.

Beast: Deep down, your fear that nothing you do is ever quite good enough leads you on an unquenchable quest for perfection. Perfectionism is a personality trait in which a person strives for flawlessness and sets standards that are nearly impossible to achieve. It is often characterized by self-criticism and a fear of criticism by others.

After a certain point, the time invested in further perfecting the goal does not prove worthy. So as a perfectionist, you often make things more difficult or complicated than is necessary to get to the objective.

OVERACHIEVING

Beauty: You are good at getting things done. You like to check to-dos off your list. And you especially like the feeling of accomplishing important goals. You are a doer and this serves you, your family, your coworkers, and others very well.

Beast: You almost always do more than is required and are driven by external accolades and praise. You may even get an emotional boost from the feeling that you have surpassed others. You are rarely satisfied that you have enough. This is partly because achievements have become a source of validation and acceptance. Even when accomplishments no longer hold meaning, you may continue to pursue them out of insecurity or a need for acceptance, making it less likely you'll choose what's meaningful.

OVER-RESPONSIBILITY

Beauty: You are super reliable. You think ahead about what might go wrong and put things in place to keep those scenarios from happening. You are quick to help out. You don't just know your job or role, but you know what everyone else should be doing as well. Everyone knows that if you are involved, nothing will fall through the cracks.

Beast: Taking ownership of your responsibilities is a hallmark of successful adulthood, but you don't just take responsibility for your own tasks—you take on other people's as well. It's called *over-responsibility*. You consistently do for others what they can do for themselves, so they often don't take responsibility if you're around. You stress about whether people in your life will hold up their end of the bargain, so you step in to take on tasks that aren't yours.

APPROVAL ADDICTION

Beauty: You are great at listening to the needs of others. You are considerate and easy to get along with. You are likeable and rarely cause problems for others. You go out of your way to be nice. Others often admire the things you work hard to accomplish.

Beast: Saying no to people makes you very anxious. You avoid conversations and situations where you think you will disappoint others. You hide information about yourself that you think will result in disapproval from others. Your decisions are often influenced by a fear of rejection or fear of what others might think. This impacts your ability to conquer time tyranny because you don't want to disappoint or upset anyone by turning down their requests. *No* is a powerful word, but only if you use it.

MISPLACED GUILT

Beauty: You have a strong sense of fairness. You like to do what is right. If you do something wrong or someone is hurt inadvertently by your actions, you are quick to apologize and make amends. Guilt is a healthy emotion when you've done something wrong. It means you have a conscience.

Beast: You feel guilty about others' choices and things you have not actually done wrong. As a result, you overcompensate and over-commit in ways you do not have time for. And if you have manipulative people in your life who understand you possess this vulnerability, they can use it to get you to choose the false urgencies they want you to focus on rather than the meaningful choices that will bring peace, purpose, and happiness.

EXTERNAL INFLUENCERS: THE DISTRACTIONS THAT IMPACT ALL OF US

In addition to the Core Vulnerabilities that impact us all in varying degrees, there are also three external influencers that everyone has to navigate in today's world. We've talked about these, but now I want to explicitly identify them as types of vulnerability you must learn to conquer. They are psychological vulnerabilities that are often manipulated by traditional and social media, and they can become major time stealers if you do not reclaim control of your thoughts.

SCREEN SEDUCTION

Our brains are wired for information and rewards. Even virtual ones release a shot of dopamine, such as when we do the following:

1. Seek and almost instantaneously find information.
2. Get the reward of a "like," a new follower, or achieving the next level on our favorite game.
3. Satisfy our urges with a quick online purchase.

SOCIAL STATUS

Social status impacts time and happiness in the modern world in three distinct ways:

1. Busyness has become a status symbol that has come to signal that someone is important, in demand, and even financially prosperous.
2. The quest for material possessions can put you into a vicious cycle of working more in order to pay for things that boost your perceived status.
3. Fear of rejection or disapproval can lead you to take on activities and say yes to requests in order to stay in the good graces of others.

TECH ADAPTATION

Because technology is constantly expanding, so is our reliance on it. These are two ways that happens:

1. As we are introduced to new technology, it becomes our new normal and we raise our expectations of how much we can accomplish in a given amount of time.
2. Rather than using technology to save time, we end up using it to cram more activity into our days (the efficiency treadmill).

#MEANINGFULOVERURGENT

OVERCOMING YOUR VULNERABILITIES

Overcoming your vulnerabilities requires two skills:

1. The mindfulness to notice when you are at risk of choosing the urgent over the meaningful
2. The ability to coach yourself toward the solution that is timeless—one you won't later regret, but instead will appreciate

Here's an example of my Core Vulnerabilities at work, and the mindfulness and self-coaching skills that can help conquer those vulnerabilities.

I had just pulled into the parking lot at the office when I heard my text message chime. I turned off the car and reached for my phone to see who it was, assuming the text was from one of the handful of people in my immediate circle. To my surprise, it was an old acquaintance I had not seen or talked to in quite some time. I've always enjoyed her company and our conversations, so when I saw her name appear on my phone, I smiled with interest. Our family's lives have kept us so busy that we rarely touch base now. Nonetheless, she's someone I respect a lot. She is accomplished and kind, resilient and full of faith.

I swiped right to open her message. It was a request to speak at an upcoming event at her church. She said it was short notice, but didn't mention how short. So I replied with a friendly "Hi" and asked her a few questions about the event. When she responded with the date, I knew in my gut it was not something I could do. I had an upcoming project with time cleared on my calendar, and if I agreed to this, I knew I would regret it.

I could feel my breathing getting shallow as I imagined the stress that would ensue as the event approached and it came time to make good on my time debt. A big part of me wanted to meet my friend's request. The event was my core audience, the church was awesome, my message could benefit them—and the request came from a personal connection.

There was a time when this sort of request would have been almost an automatic yes for me. I would have considered it an investment because perhaps I'd be invited back for a bigger event later. That is how I built my business. My optimism to believe that one opportunity could lead to another had worked well over the years.

I didn't want to say no via text, and since she asked for a phone meeting, I agreed to call the next morning. I felt some anxiety because I knew she would be hopeful that I could do the event. I had a knot in the pit of my stomach. My question was: How do I turn down the request?

That night I decided to script my rejection. I identified what was creating my anxiety, and I addressed each point. Here are the fears I uncovered through self-reflection that were bubbling up and causing me to feel anxious:

- My friend would be offended, and it would negatively impact our future relationship.
- Since I did not have another actual event that day, I was somehow being disingenuous by saying I was not available.
- If I said no now, her church would never invite me again, so I would miss out on future opportunities.
- I might be perceived as dismissive, unappreciative, or arrogant, as though I thought I was above the request.

Writing out my unvarnished thoughts was extremely helpful for self-reflection. By taking a pause to question my anxiety, I was able to face it and get unstuck. I read my list of fears several times. Then one by one, I began to tell the truth about those fears. I had to say no, if

I was to be fair to my future self and honest about my needs. I could not succumb to fear or unbridled optimism and convince myself I had the time to say yes to the request.

Fear #1: My friend would be offended, and it would damage our relationship.

> **Truth:** *She is a professional and a mom. This is no big deal to her. She understands having a schedule full of commitments. If she is offended and treats me differently for honoring my own needs, she is not the woman I thought she was. I don't think she'll do that.*

Fear #2: Because I don't have another event that day, it is disingenuous to say I'm not available.

> **Truth:** *A commitment is an event. You need to redefine what constitutes a legitimate conflict. Just because you don't have a physical place you must be that day does not mean you don't have a schedule conflict.*

Fear #3: By saying no, I'll miss out on future invitations.

> **Truth:** *Maybe. Maybe not. I cannot let fear of missing out guide my decisions. Period.*

Fear #4: I'll be perceived as dismissive, unappreciative, or arrogant.

> **Truth:** *That's ridiculous. I'm not any of those things. If I were, I wouldn't be sitting here fretting over saying no! I'd have texted no and kept moving with my day.*

As you can see, after taking less than five minutes to notice the thoughts I was having that created the anxiety, I was able to consider whether each thought was truth or just fear. From there, I was able to jot down what I wanted to say on the call the next day. There were about four things I wanted to convey. It looked something like this:

- "Thank you so much for the invitation. I loved speaking there before and would love to speak again."
- "The thing is, I am working on a project that is due right around that time. I will stress myself out trying to do both, and possibly put my commitment to the project in jeopardy. I don't want to say no, but I really have to."
- "If you're doing the event again next year, I'd love to see if the calendar lines up then."
- "It's been so long since we got together. We need to put a date on our calendars for after my project is done, if you have some time."

To my utter delight, her response was beautiful and unexpected. "You know, Valorie," she said, "I have so much respect for how you are honoring your commitments. I know you have a lot of requests, and I know it is hard sometimes. I know it's hard for me. But honestly, it is inspiring how you are able to say no graciously. I totally understand, and I really appreciate you considering the event."

My jaw literally dropped. Here I was anxious about saying no, and she was telling me she respected how I declined? It was both confirmation and encouragement.

The two Core Vulnerabilities that threatened to sabotage me that day were tidsoptimism (adding the event to my already full schedule on short notice would have caused a great deal of stress, but my first thought was to tell myself I could find a way to do it even though I knew I didn't have the time) and approval addiction (I was riddled with thoughts about how saying no would be perceived).

What are your vulnerabilities? Let's take a moment now to assess that question.

Vulnerabilities Assessment

I have identified six Core Vulnerabilities that impact your relationship with time:

1. Tidsoptimism
2. Overachievement
3. Over-responsibility
4. Guilt
5. Perfectionism
6. Approval addiction

There are three other external vulnerabilities that also affect your relationship with time:

1. Screen seduction
2. Social status
3. Tech addiction

Read each of the following statements and choose the answer that sounds most like you. If you feel stuck, go with your gut response. Don't think too hard about your answers.

1. You get done with an appointment an hour earlier than expected. Your very first thought is . . .
   a. I can squeeze in some errands before I pick up the kids.
   b. Oh good, that'll give me a little extra time so I don't have to rush.

2. A neighbor tells you she turned down a promotion at work because she didn't want the added responsibility even though she'd get a 25 percent raise and a sought-after position. You . . .

    a. Wonder why she works so hard if she doesn't want to get ahead.

    b. Admire her willingness to turn down the job and the clarity she has about her vision.

3. Your twelve-year-old tends to be scattered and forgetful. Today she texts you after you drop her off at school to tell you she left an assignment in your car. You . . .

    a. Tell her to tell her teacher what happened and that she will bring it the next day.

    b. Feel bad that you can't get back to the school right now, but decide to scan the assignment and email it to her teacher.

4. A friend asks you to attend an event this Sunday, but you had planned to spend that day catching up on some much-needed rest. You . . .

    a. Feel selfish for wanting to decline because she always says yes to anything you ask of her. You say yes.

    b. Tell her how worn down you feel this week and hope she understands.

5. You check your phone for email or social media within fifteen minutes of waking up.

    a. Never.

    b. Most days or every day.

6. You post something on your favorite social media platform about the fun concert you went to this weekend. Thirty minutes later, no one has liked or commented on your status. You . . .

    a. Feel a bit dejected and contemplate deleting the post.

b. Don't notice because you've already started doing something else and haven't gone back to check the post yet.

7. You are going on vacation and are worried about the number of emails that will pile up while you're gone. You . . .
   a. Take your laptop with you and plan to spend only twenty minutes per day checking in so the messages don't pile up.
   b. Dread the pile of emails that you'll face when you get back, but leave the laptop behind anyway.

8. You pull up to the coffee shop to meet a friend ten minutes after you said you would. You think to yourself . . .
   a. Why does it always seem like no matter what, I'm ten minutes late? Ugh.
   b. I really misjudged my time today.

9. You look at your to-do list near the end of the day. You can only check off half the items, but it occurs to you that you finished some tasks that were not on the list. The next thing you do is . . .
   a. Add the tasks to the list and check them off!
   b. Begin working on the next task you can cross off.

10. You and your spouse are a dual-income household. When it comes to scheduling family appointments, gatherings, or other needs, which is true?
    a. It is a joint effort or your spouse handles it.
    b. You handle the scheduling and planning because your spouse isn't good at it or doesn't want to do it.

11. You are a single parent to your son, and his other parent lives in another town. You get an email asking one parent per

household to volunteer for a school event in the middle of a
school day.

   a. You feel overwhelmed with guilt that your child won't have
      a parent there because you can't get off work. You pick
      up the latest game your son wants and surprise him with
      it as consolation.

   b. You reply that you wish you could volunteer that day, but
      your schedule won't permit it. You don't buy him a gift as
      consolation.

12. When you log into your social media accounts, you spend
more time than you intended.

   a. Very rarely.

   b. Most of the time or all of the time.

13. You are at a dinner party and the conversation turns to what
everyone has been up to. A woman next to you begins going
on about all the projects on her plate and her trip out of town
next week. You . . .

   a. Think she sounds important, and you start thinking of
      the important things you are doing that you could talk
      about.

   b. Start asking her questions about her travel or projects.

14. The holidays are coming up, and you are excited about
how much time you'll save by shopping online. As a
result, you . . .

   a. End up waiting until the last minute. It won't take as long,
      so there's no need to get started too early.

   b. Shop online around the same time you used to shop in
      stores. You get your shopping done faster and feel more
      relaxed than usual during the holiday season.

15. When you look at the calendar and see that there is more to do than most people would think is possible, you tend to think . . .

   a. I am more efficient than the average person, and there's a way to do this.

   b. Something has to go. I can't do all this.

16. When people seem in awe of your accomplishments, you feel . . .

   a. Special. You do more than the average person, and it feels affirming when others recognize this unique trait.

   b. Pleased. It is nice of them to compliment you on your accomplishments.

17. You often find yourself frustrated by a fellow committee member in your volunteer group who does not pull his weight. You . . .

   a. Bring up your needs to him and ask when he plans to complete his part of the project. You refuse to keep up with your responsibilities and his.

   b. Tell yourself it's not that big of a deal. It'll be easier to just do the tasks yourself than to cause conflict.

18. Your sister asks you at the last minute to babysit for the weekend so she can go away on a romantic trip, but you already have plans. She reminds you how lucky you are that your time is all yours because you don't have children.

   a. You feel bad that she never gets time for herself and cancel your plans. If you say no, you'll not only get an earful from her, but from your parents too.

   b. You tell her you can help out one night, but she'll need to ask someone else to help the second night.

19. I feel anxious if I don't have my phone with me, like I am missing something.
    a. This does not describe me at all.
    b. This describes me.

20. Your daughter wants to participate in band, dance, and a local theater group simultaneously. It is a lot, but two of her best friends are doing the same three activities. You . . .
    a. Don't want her to be the only one who doesn't get to do the activities she loves, so you say yes.
    b. Tell her it is too much at once and let her choose her favorite one or two activities.

21. You have a friend who calls when she has a routine question. She never texts. You are . . .
    a. Irritated that she calls for trivial questions when she could just text you. You've started replying to her incoming calls with a text message. It's much faster.
    b. Amused and find it kind of endearing that she calls so often. You answer the phone pretty much anytime she calls.

22. Your kids are old enough to fold towels and sheets, but they are just plain awful at it, and everything ends up looking jumbled and messy in the linen closet. You . . .
    a. Have them do it anyway.
    b. Assign them another chore and do the folding yourself. It's faster and it looks better.

23. Your neighbor invites you to a party where her sister is selling products from her business that you have no interest in. It looks like at least three other neighbors are going, and they've all asked if you'll be there. You . . .

a. Decide to attend because you feel bad saying no when you'll be sitting in the house right next door and you don't have any plans anyway.

b. Thank her for the invitation and say you won't be attending.

24. There's a job available that you'd love to have, but you are disappointed because after reading the qualifications, you only have a little over half of them. You . . .

a. Feel your heart sink as you read the list. You plan to get some more experience and apply when it comes open again in the future.

b. Apply for the job. You can learn the other skills if given the chance.

25. You started a new job at your company and have been assigned a project that is taking a long time to figure out. A coworker you don't know well has done it before, but they appear very busy. You . . .

a. Are sure you can figure it out and decide to spend a little more time doing so. You don't want to come across as incompetent or bother them.

b. Ask the coworker to show you how to do it even though they are busy.

26. You are working on something creative—a drawing, a piece of writing, or a design of some sort. It has been a while and your family and friends keep bugging you to let them see your progress. You . . .

a. Tell them it isn't ready yet. You don't want anyone to see until it's good enough to show. Why do they keep asking?

b. Show it to anyone willing to take a look. You want feedback.

27. You spent an excessive amount of time getting ready for a school reunion—choosing your clothes, grooming, etc. The most likely reason is . . .
    a. You were just moving slowly for some reason today.
    b. Your ex is going to be there and you want to make sure he sees how amazing you look these days.

Determining Your Core Vulnerabilities

To determine which of the vulnerabilities you possess or lean toward, use the chart below.

1. a = 3 points, b = 0 points
2. a = 3 points, b = 0 points
3. a = 0 points, b = 3 points
4. a = 3 points, b = 0 points
5. a = 0 points, b = 3 points
6. a = 3 points, b = 0 points
7. a = 3 points, b = 0 points
8. a = 3 points, b = 0 points
9. a = 3 points, b = 0 points
10. a = 0 points, b = 3 points
11. a = 3 points, b = 0 points
12. a = 0 points, b = 3 points
13. a = 3 points, b = 0 points
14. a = 3 points, b = 0 points
15. a = 3 points, b = 0 points
16. a = 3 points, b = 0 points
17. a = 0 points, b = 3 points
18. a = 3 points, b = 0 points
19. a = 0 points, b = 3 points

20. a = 3 points, b = 0 points
21. a = 3 points, b = 0 points
22. a = 0 points, b = 3 points
23. a = 3 points, b = 0 points
24. a = 3 points, b = 0 points
25. a = 3 points, b = 0 points
26. a = 3 points, b = 0 points
27. a = 0 points, b = 3 points

Tidsoptimism

Add up your points from questions 1, 8, and 15.

If your score is 9, it is a Core Vulnerability.

If your score is 6, you lean toward this vulnerability.

If you scored 0–3, this is not a vulnerability for you.

Overachievement

Add up your points from questions 2, 9, and 16.

If your score is 9, it is a Core Vulnerability.

If your score is 6, you lean toward this vulnerability.

If you scored 0–3, this is not a vulnerability for you.

Over-Responsibility

Add up your points from questions 3, 10, and 17.

If your score is 9, it is a Core Vulnerability.

If your score is 6, you lean toward this vulnerability.

If you scored 0–3, this is not a vulnerability for you.

Guilt

Add up your points from questions 4, 11, and 18.

If your score is 9, it is a Core Vulnerability.

If your score is 6, you lean toward this vulnerability.

If you scored 0–3, this is not a vulnerability for you.

Perfectionism

Add up your points from questions 22, 24, and 26.

If your score is 9, it is a Core Vulnerability.

If your score is 6, you lean toward this vulnerability.

If you scored 0–3, this is not a vulnerability for you.

Approval Addiction

Add up your points from questions 23, 25, and 27.

If your score is 9, it is a Core Vulnerability.

If your score is 6, you lean toward this vulnerability.

If you scored 0–3, this is not a vulnerability for you.

Screen Seduction

Add up your points from questions 5, 12, and 19.

If your score is 9, it is a Core Vulnerability.

If your score is 6, you lean toward this vulnerability.

If you scored 0–3, this is not a vulnerability for you.

Social Status

Add up your points from questions 6, 13, and 20.

If your score is 9, it is a Core Vulnerability.

If your score is 6, you lean toward this vulnerability.

If you scored 0–3, this is not a vulnerability for you.

Tech Adaptation

Add up your points from questions 7, 14, and 21.

If your score is 9, it is a Core Vulnerability.

If your score is 6, you lean toward this vulnerability.

If you scored 0–3, this is not a vulnerability for you.

You now know your personal vulnerabilities. Consider your most pressing time demand and which vulnerabilities make it harder for you to overcome it. The actions and questions below are a coaching tool. Answer the questions that correlate with your vulnerabilities to coach yourself to engage in actions and shifts that will help you break free.

COACHING TOOLBOX

Strategies to Combat Core Vulnerabilities

When you feel your core vulnerabilities influencing your decision, use these strategies to overcome them and make wise, meaningful choices with your time.

Tidsoptimism

- Put on your pessimistic hat and look for what might not go as planned. Decide how you'd handle the challenge.
- Talk to a more pessimistic peer who may be able to see the negatives that are hard for you to see right now.
- Give yourself extra time even if you don't think you need it. If your optimism was right, you'll be in great shape. If your optimism was wrong, you'll be grateful for the buffer.

Perfectionism

- Give yourself permission to be imperfect. Decide what "good enough" is before you get started, and when you get to good enough, declare yourself finished and move on. "Good enough" can be a high standard, but don't make it an impossible standard.
- Trust that progress is a process, and focus on learning and growing more than reaching a destination or beating a time clock.
- When you notice yourself being self-critical, pause. Then intentionally switch to self-compassion: Acknowledge your effort and progress. Talk to yourself the way you'd talk to someone you care about. Be kind to yourself.

Overachieving

- Remind yourself that achievements do not make you more valuable. Your worth is not tied to what you do.
- Crave purpose, not praise. Be honest with yourself when you take on commitments. Ensure that you are doing something because it is meaningful, not because of the external accolades you'll receive.
- Decide what area of your life is worth the extra effort and in what area you'd rather be a deliberate "underachiever." If you're going to *be* a high achiever, do it strategically.

Over-Responsibility

- Let others take responsibility for themselves. Stop reminding, prodding, or taking over.
- Be willing to let the ball drop when the outcome is not your responsibility. Allow others to experience the consequences of their behavior so they can grow and change.
- Add up the time you would save if you stopped doing what someone else is responsible for. Then ask, "What might be a more meaningful use of that saved time?"

Approval Addiction

- Realize that saying no when you need to allows you to say yes to what matters.
- Get comfortable with being uncomfortable. Say no and refuse to let your emotions rule your decisions.
- Don't take rejection personally, and remember there is no badge for going it alone. Be willing to ask for help if it will save you time.

Misplaced Guilt

- Refuse to be manipulated by guilt. If you sense that is what's happening as you are making a time choice, step away. Say,

"Let me get back to you." Removing yourself from the conversation will help you get your thoughts and words together.

- Guilt is about doing something wrong. Clarify what is right and what is wrong.
- Once you correct a mistake or fault, refuse to further overcompensate or waste time proving yourself. Let it go. Learn from it. Move forward.

PQs to Combat External Influencers

Powerful Questions, or PQs, are tools you can use to dig beneath the surface of challenges to shed light on critical information and help you find potential solutions. Consider a pressing time demand that is made worse by your vulnerability to one of the external influencers. Use the PQs below to help coach yourself to reduce the impact.

Screen Seduction PQs

- Is the choice to engage with the screen right now moving me closer to my desired goal or farther from it?
- What can I do right now to redirect my attention to my immediate, physical environment (as opposed to a virtual one)?
- What can I do to restrict my access to screens right now?

Social Status PQs

- What choice would I make if I was not concerned about the reactions, approval, or admiration of others?
- Is this decision based on social pressure or authentic relationship-building?
- What is the real source of my value, significance, and worth?
- If I made the most authentic and wise choice, what would it be?

Tech Adaptation PQs

- What time has this technology or advancement saved me that I did not have before?
- What is the best use of the saved time I gained from this technology or advancement?
- If I must now do more in less time, what adjustments can I make to minimize the stress of adapting to the heightened expectation?

This type of self-reflective coaching takes practice. It isn't something you do once but instead something you incorporate into your routine. The busier and more demanding your schedule, the more important it is that you are aware of your vulnerabilities and take steps to minimize their impact on your time choices.

. . . .

MEANINGFUL MINUTE

When we acknowledge our fears, we can shed light on them and move forward with powerful answers rooted in truth. Coaching yourself through your fears is freeing.

Describe a specific situation in which fear is tempting you to commit time when the wise choice would be to reserve the time for more meaningful matters.

_____

_____

_____

Name your fears and the truths that counter each one.

Fear #1:

_____

Truth:

_____

Fear #2:

_____

Truth:

_____

What is the most meaningful use of your time in this situation?

_____

CHAPTER TEN

PRESS PAUSE

Jamie had been home for about twenty minutes and was scrolling through Facebook when one of her children ran into the kitchen and asked, "What's for dinner, Mom?" She felt a pang of guilt as she quickly laid her phone on the counter and pretended she wasn't engrossed in her news feed. Jamie needed to get dinner started, but she was distracted—and exhausted. Even though it was a simple question, it tipped Jamie over the edge.

"You'll find out what's for dinner when I put it on the table!" she snapped.

Her daughter looked at her blankly, then shrugged, turned, and skipped into the living room to announce to her older siblings, "Mom said we'll find out when we get to the table!"

It wasn't the first time Jamie had lost her cool over her kids' constant stream of questions and requests at the end of a long day. She felt exhausted by the need to have answers for everything, and truth be told, she had not yet figured out what was for dinner, even though she was hungry too. Scrolling through Facebook was a mindless distraction from that reality. But her daughter's innocent and reasonable question left Jamie feeling condemned and overwhelmed.

In the background, she could hear that she'd received two text messages and an email chime. She wanted to resist the urge to check her phone, but she didn't. She impulsively grabbed it as she always did. The texts were from a neighbor asking if she'd decided whether she could help with the neighborhood holiday party and reminding her of the dates again. It was another decision she needed to make. The other was from her boss asking if it still looked like she'd be able to meet a deadline for a report later that week. Should she answer or should she avoid opening the full text and pretend she hadn't read it yet? Yet one more decision.

You probably picked up on Jamie's vulnerabilities of screen seduction and guilt. Add to that the decision fatigue, and she really needs a tool that can help her choose well even when she feels stressed and pressed for time.

PRACTICE THE POWER OF A PAUSE

When we are overwhelmed, the wisest choice is to pause. But instead, we often just keep running on autopilot, driven by time tyranny, which tells us we don't have time to pause and make an intentional choice. But that is actually when we most need to do exactly those things. The practice of stopping and taking stock of the situation is called mindfulness.

When there are too many demands for your brain's attention, the amygdala (the part of your brain that processes memory, decisions, and emotions) gets overwhelmed.[1] Pausing to focus on the present moment calms your mind and allows you to think more clearly. When that happens, it is easier to choose the meaningful over the seemingly urgent. There are many simple acts that can bring us into the present moment fairly quickly, but doing so requires your intention and attention. And you may find yourself being easily drawn away by your smartphone, emails, and other distractions, just as Jamie was.

Mindfulness is mental training. It is learning to turn off your autopilot and take control of your thoughts. The key to mindfulness is to practice. The point at which you notice you are not being mindful is the point at which you become mindful. You noticed you were not in the present moment. That's a good thing—don't beat yourself up! Just get back on track. Little wins build your confidence. Consider these simple acts of mindfulness to get started.

1. **Breathe deeply.** Sit up straight, close your eyes, inhale for four seconds, and exhale for eight seconds. Repeat the inhale and exhale five times. Focus your thoughts entirely on your breathing. Notice what the air feels like moving through your body. Feel the sensation of your abdomen as it rises and falls. Research has repeatedly shown that this simple exercise, and variations of it, can lower stress, anxiety, and negative emotion, and increase your attention span.[2]

2. **Put your feet on the ground.** To feel more grounded and present, literally put your feet on the ground. Whether you are having an important phone conversation or making a decision, sitting with both feet on the ground or standing with your feet evenly centered can be powerful. Even better, go outside and let your bare feet touch the grass or soil beneath you.

3. **Name that sound.** Quiet yourself and notice the sounds around you, which will awaken your senses to your immediate environment. When we are on autopilot we often do not notice the sounds in our environment. Bring yourself into the present by noticing how many sounds you can name, whether it's the fan whirring in the background, birds chirping as the sun rises, or the neighbors' kids playing in the distance.

4. **Do a body scan.** Most of the time we are unaware of our bodies—the tensions we hold, our postures, and even sensations we're feeling. Bring yourself into the present moment by mindfully giving your attention to each area of your body—head

to toe. It takes just a minute. Sit or lie down, and begin by wiggling your toes and moving your feet. Move up to your legs and knees, then thighs and hips. Intentionally relax the muscles as you scan. Notice the movement of your abdomen and then chest as you breathe. Relax your arms and shoulders. Stretch your neck. Relax your jaw and then your eyes and forehead. And finally, notice any sensations at the top of your head. This is a simple way to bring your focus to the present moment.

5. **Shift from "have to" to "get to."** One simple act of mindfulness is to express gratitude by adjusting your description of what's on your schedule for the day. Most of us talk about what we "have to" do. "I have to go to work." "I have to go grocery shopping." "I have to take my child to sports practice." When you shift your words to "get to," you become mindful of the gift in each item on your list. You *get to* go to work. That means you have a paying job. Somebody surely would love that opportunity. You *get to* go grocery shopping. That means you have the resources to buy food for your household. You *get to* take your child to practice. That means she is healthy enough to play a sport. This simple change in language raises your awareness of your blessings right here in the moment.

6. **Empathize.** When we are busy or feel overwhelmed, we lose our ability to empathize. It is one of the ways bandwidth poverty plagues us. You are so emotionally absorbed by your own demands that your capacity to feel for others becomes diminished. Pausing to intentionally notice and meet the needs of other people—by getting them a cup of coffee or lending a listening ear, for example—helps you tap into the well of compassion that reconnects you with others.

7. **Eat slowly.** When hurried, eating becomes a mindless chore. When mindful, it becomes a source of joy and an opportunity to slow down. During your next meal or snack, eat slowly,

notice the textures and flavors of your food as you chew, pause between bites, and savor.

8. **Get moving.** Exercise pulls you into the present moment as you become aware of your body. Even two minutes of exercise, from marching in place to jumping jacks or dancing, can immediately shift your mood to a more positive state. The key is to raise your heart rate, which can trigger neurotransmitters such as serotonin and dopamine that make you feel good.

9. **Listen mindfully.** In your next conversation, intentionally listen with the goal of allowing other people to feel heard. Forget about asserting your opinion or countering their points or sharing your story. Instead, listen to their words, their voice tone, their body language, and their emotion. Hear them. Suspend judgment. Listen with love. In today's hurried world, it is a gift. Few people ever feel truly heard.

SIX EXERCISES TO BUILD YOUR WILLPOWER

Being mindful gives us a greater ability to deal with the ever-increasing onslaught of technology and choices that characterize our lives. Stanford researcher Kelly McGonigal, author of *The Willpower Instinct*, describes willpower as a muscle that can be strengthened through training and exercise.[3] Practice the mindfulness ideas I shared on preceding pages to build up your mindfulness muscles, and consider the following strategies to specifically strengthen your willpower in those moments when you need to overcome Core Vulnerabilities, resist distractions, or make one more decision despite experiencing decision fatigue.

- Make decisions about your schedule early in the week, early in the day, or early in the meeting, before making other decisions.

Your decision-making muscle gets fatigued, so aim to make important decisions before that happens.

- Eliminate as many choices and decisions as possible by automating, delegating, or delaying them. Automate the decisions that don't need consistent attention. Delegate as many as possible by training others in an effective decision-making process. Delay decisions that you do not yet have enough information to effectively make.

- Don't resist your cravings; redirect them. Sit quietly and picture yourself in the heat of the moment when you feel compelled to reach for your phone and open your favorite social media app for the fifth time today. What are you really craving when you compulsively open the app? What is the feeling that leads you to that solution? If it is feeling connected, for example, identify a more meaningful way to connect—maybe call a friend, talk with someone right there in your immediate surroundings, or send a heartfelt and personal thank-you to someone who's helped you. Identify your two or three most tempting time stealers. Then identify in advance what you will do instead when the temptation arises.

- Eat well and on time. Low blood sugar and physical fatigue lower willpower. People with low blood sugar are more impulsive, take more risks, and are more likely to give in to temptations. Scientists speculate that this could be because low blood sugar throws your body into survival mode, making it more likely for you to take risks.[4] Also, stress hormones increase when blood sugar drops, and stress depletes self-control.[5] So avoid skipping meals or snacks, and if your blood sugar gets low, eat a piece of fruit or drink juice or fat-free milk. Your blood sugar should begin to rise within about ten minutes.

- Sleep plenty. A lack of sleep can also wear down your willpower muscle by making it harder to process decisions. Getting a full night's sleep will help keep your mind clear and help you deal better with stress.

- Do ten minutes of deep-breathing. One of the exercises I shared earlier in the chapter is a one-minute breathing exercise. Make it a goal to increase the amount of time you are able to do it. The longer you are able to focus your energy on calming, rhythmic breathing, the more you exercise your mindfulness skills—and that builds willpower.
- Laugh. Count your blessings. Do something fun. Positive emotion has been shown to restore your ability to exert willpower. So be intentional about cultivating positive emotion.[6] Take a break and play. Stop and reflect on what you're grateful for and why—even write down your blessings. Talk to a funny friend or watch something that makes you laugh.

When Jamie got frustrated and snapped at her daughter, her willpower was depleted from a day of nonstop decision-making and trying her best to stay focused even though her smartphone apps gave her what felt like a mental reprieve. There's a good chance her blood sugar was low, since it had been hours since lunch. Whatever the reasons for her energy crash, it felt like she was barely making it to the finish line at the end of the day. And her family was getting the short end of the stick, which also left her feeling guilty.

During a coaching session, she acknowledged that her two older kids seemed to be less open with her than they used to be. She was concerned about the change and did not want to remain on autopilot with her habits. It was becoming a running joke that she was "addicted" to her phone. She wasn't happy and often felt like time was slipping through her fingers.

Sometimes you have to simply stop and remind yourself of what is important to you and what you need in order to be able to focus on what matters. In Jamie's case, we came up with a few ideas. She decided to keep a snack box in her car so that she was not so hungry when she walked in the door in the evenings. And she would leave her phone in the car for the first hour after she arrived home. Since two of her kids were over the age of twelve, she delegated dinner to them two nights a week to give herself a break and engage her kids with contributing more to the household. They could choose what to make, but they had to plan in advance so that the items needed were on the grocery list for the week.

And she decided to try an experiment for one week. She gave herself a few moments to transition from her day to her evening by taking a walk alone around the block and then connecting with her family in conversation when she got back. She made a point of looking them in the eye, listening, and being present. At the end of that week, she felt more relaxed and connected. And the more she showed up fully, the more her children opened up and talked about what was going on with them. All of these changes happened when she turned off autopilot, paused, and focused on what was meaningful.

· ·

MEANINGFUL MINUTE

Every time you need to make a choice that will impact how you spend your time, *pause*. Then ask yourself . . .

Is this choice meaningful, or is this choice a false urgency, a distraction from a more meaningful use of my time?

_____

_____

Looking back later, what is the choice I will wish I had made?

_____

_____

CHAPTER ELEVEN

THE TEMPERAMENT TO EXPERIMENT

I just want to take a moment to congratulate you. You have made it through a lot of pages. We've talked about the problem of time tyranny, the history of how we got here, and the challenges that tend to get us stuck. I know you are serious about making some changes in your life, because you're still here! You've probably already begun to shift your thinking about time, and perhaps even made some shifts in how you approach it. Now, in these last two chapters, you are going to decide exactly what change looks like in this season of your life and then make it happen.

Here's the thing: there are lots of options for change. But how do you know what will stick? What will deliver the meaning and time you long for? Often, you don't know. What you think will work sometimes doesn't. What you think won't work sometimes is just the change you need. So here's what I propose: *Experiment.* Try out some possibilities. See how they impact you. Notice what works. Do more of it. Notice what doesn't. Tweak it or drop it altogether.

When I began this journey, I desperately wanted change, but I was at a loss as to what to do. If I had been coaching someone else, the path forward may have been clearer to me. But I knew my habits, and they were so deeply ingrained, I did not have definite answers. So I decided to do something I have done with many of my clients over the years: rather than making grand declarations about what I was going to do "from now on," I tried "experiments." This is a way to try out new ideas and see where they lead. It's like shopping and trying on an outfit to see how it looks. The experimental approach "tries out" new behaviors and then uses the tool of self-reflection to create a plan that will get you to the transformation you desire.

If you are willing to develop a temperament to experiment rather than make broad declarations about permanent changes, you give yourself the flexibility to create change that is sustainable and meaningful for you and those you care about. This approach can be fun too. It certainly has been for me and my family. You can brainstorm. Try out an experiment for a day or a week or a month or even a year. It just depends on the circumstances.

Here are some simple rules to help you develop a temperament to experiment. Jeff and I used these to develop our experiments. Feel free to tweak these or add your own rules:

- Identify the time challenges that stress or frustrate you most.
- Ask: What could I do differently that might solve this challenge or have a positive impact on alleviating the stress or frustration of this challenge?
- Create parameters for trying out the idea that are specific and actionable.
- Give the experiment a time frame.
- Set a reminder at the end of the time frame to reflect on the experiment and ask the following PQs:

- Did it improve my relationship with time? How so?
- Did it change my life in a meaningful way? How so?
- What worked well?
- What didn't work well? How could I change or tweak what didn't work well?
- Do I want to turn this experiment into a permanent change?

THE BIG CALENDAR "EXPERIMENT"

One of our early experiments unfolded organically. Around the time I read the *New York Times* article that let me know I was living in time poverty, I went to Jacksonville, Florida, to speak at Celebration Church for Mother's Day weekend. While there, I had lunch with co-pastor Kerri Weems, who casually mentioned her calendar after I described some of my challenges with time. She wrote a book called *Rhythms of Grace*, and I knew she'd have some wisdom to share. Sometimes you need to hear the perspective of someone you admire who has dealt with similar challenges—maybe even bigger ones—and conquered them. It can inspire you to action.

With three children, a large church, and writing and speaking commitments, Kerri and her husband, Stovall Weems, had a lot going on. So she and Pastor Stovall planned a year in advance on a calendar with all of their kids' school calendars and commitments, her and her husband's commitments, and the church calendar. Everyone met to discuss the calendar, what activities could be undertaken, and which ones could not. I was intrigued. I kept a calendar, of course, but nothing as big picture as she described.

When I got home, we decided to create our own whole-year calendar. We picked up a year-at-a-glance wall calendar and began filling in everything—family birthdays, school calendars for the kids, summer camps, confirmed speaking engagements, holidays, family reunions, coach training weekends, scheduled trips, anniversaries, everything we could think of.

Then a glaring reality hit us. It was almost June. Summer had arrived. Neighbors and family were leaving for vacation, and we didn't have one planned. Jeff had not been given any of the summer vacation dates he'd requested—one of the hard realities of working in the aviation industry. Summertime means more flights. He was flying everyone else on their vacations but unable to schedule one for himself. We were a few years into our marriage, and I had kind of just accepted the idea that we can't plan a vacation because my husband doesn't have much control over his vacation time. I adjusted my time off to his, even if the dates didn't work well for a vacation because of school calendars or weather.

Creating a whole-year calendar raised the question: When can *we* take a break?

What we discovered was that we had casually filled up our schedules and now there was no room for a weeklong vacation before school started again. It was disappointing, and I felt a bit ridiculous. "How does a mom of three not plan any better than this?" I started to berate myself. But then I pivoted to a better idea.

We decided to plan something fun and memorable for the following year and chose a cruise twelve months away. We'd take two weeks off, something neither of us had ever done in our adult lives. We told our family about our plans. They decided they wanted to go too! The whole trip was even more meaningful, as we visited places we've wanted to visit for years with our children, my mom and aunt, and Jeff's dad and stepmother.

We also realized that we'd allowed Jeff's prohibitive work schedule to prevent us from planning time off together. So we asked ourselves: "How can we have a vacation without knowing whether Jeff can get the days off?"

"I can drop trips," he said, meaning that if he didn't get the days off he requested, he could give up those assigned trips on his work schedule, let another captain fly them, and not be paid for them. While foregoing pay is not ideal, it is an option, which is better than no option at all. So we decided to view this option as a vacation expense. Otherwise, we'd rarely be able to plan. And it was a solution that became a breakthrough of sorts for us, because without that decision, our vacation time as a family was held hostage to whether or not he'd be granted the days we wanted.

Besides being able to plan our first two-week vacation ever, the whole-year calendar experiment helped us better plan our holidays with family. Divorced parents and blended families, some living nearby and others out-of-state, create unique challenges around the holidays. Who will be here for Thanksgiving? Who will be here for Christmas? Will we go somewhere?

The experiment organically caused us to begin putting things in motion for higher-level planning. We reached out to our parents to find out their holiday plans. We began thinking about what we wanted to do. By planning ahead, we could invite out-of-town family in plenty of time for them to make travel arrangements and take time off.

If you don't have the same dynamics in your family, these may not be your challenges, but I assure you that if you look a year into the future, you'll naturally begin to plan in a bigger-picture way. You may even begin planting seeds for ideas for the following year.

You'll be amazed at the shifts in your mind-set and changes that can happen in your schedule when you begin doing experiments. They can be small acts you try just to see how they feel. Creating a whole-year calendar is just one experiment of many. In this next section, let's explore more experiment ideas so you can consider what you might try for yourself.

SCHEDULING EXPERIMENTS

DAILY CHECK-IN

Look at your calendar and ask these questions about the next day: "What am I doing tomorrow?" (If more than one person is doing the check-in, then each person should answer this question aloud for the others.) "What else is happening tomorrow that will affect my schedule? Who's doing what? What could I do to add more meaning or joy to my day?" Be sure to check in with yourself about the current day's activities and goals as well by asking, "Did I use my time well today? How could I have used my time better?"

STAYCATION DAYS

Vacation doesn't have to be about going somewhere. Schedule days off to remain at home or at least stay in your local area. Visit museums and parks, have a picnic, go bike riding, or see a show. Do what people do when they come visit your area. And most important, relax and have fun. Pull out your calendar and identify a staycation day every season for the next year, then make a list of how you want to spend the day. In bed reading a book? A romantic day with your spouse? A visit to a historic site you've never seen? The idea is to take a break from your routine and rejuvenate without much effort.

ALLOW BOREDOM

Daydreaming. Doodling. Staring out the window. Believe it or not, boredom is really good for you. It gives you a mental break from the stimulation of technology. And neuroscience research even shows it boosts creativity.[1] Many of us behave as though we must always be doing something, even if the something we are doing is meaningless. But doing nothing at all can be purposeful, even joyful. Just don't confuse "doing nothing" with mindlessly scrolling through Instagram.

Nothing truly means *nothing*. Block some time to be bored. And just expect to feel a bit antsy at first, especially if you are used to grabbing your phone at the first sign of boredom. When you feel the itch to do something—anything—resist, and give yourself permission to just relax, be still, and notice the trivial.

TIME-REPLACEMENT EXERCISE

The challenge with change is that we often commit to ceasing a specific behavior without first identifying what that behavior will be replaced with. As a result, change becomes an exercise in willpower rather than a more fruitful redirecting of our energy.

Try this exercise: choose your biggest time stealer, then ask yourself, "What will I do instead?" Whether your time stealer is a commitment or a role, such as head of a planning committee, or something more personal like getting lost in Facebook, decide how you want to use your time once you relinquish that activity. This way you intentionally redirect the time you gain. You might spend the extra hour a week taking a Sunday afternoon nap or hanging out with a friend or loved one.

TRY THE TIME-MEANING MATRIX

When you are faced with a decision about whether something is meaningful and the right choice right now, there is a simple illustration you can refer to called a Time-Meaning Matrix. My husband and I use it to get clarity, especially when vulnerabilities begin to cloud our decision.

Here's how it works: Decide on a scale of 1 to 10 what minimum meaning the activity needs to have in order for you to do it. Then, on a scale of 1 to 10, how would you rate the level of time commitment you are willing to make? So let's say an activity must rate at least a 5 for meaningfulness and a 5 for time commitment. Anything that falls below those numbers on the following chart should be avoided.

#MEANINGFULOVERURGENT

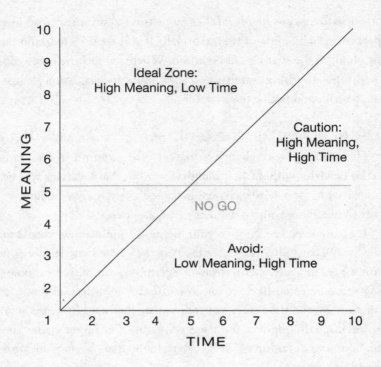

SLEEP-RESET EXPERIMENT

Feeling utterly overwhelmed on the way home from the airport, I made a decision. I would not address any of the tasks swirling in my head, despite what I had scheduled. Instead, when I got home, I would eat and then go to sleep. And while I got a little distracted by a few messages before bed, I still got to sleep far earlier than usual—around 8:30 p.m. I slept for ten hours. And when I got out of bed the next morning, something unusual happened: I felt amazing. My head was clear. My neck didn't hurt. I felt optimistic and the peaceful sensation of simply being well.

"Sleep is the new status symbol," asserts Arianna Huffington, author of *Thrive* and *The Sleep Revolution.* In today's busy world, she just might be right.

I know it sounds almost ridiculous to describe how it felt to wake up from an extra-long night's sleep, but I felt so good I was determined to figure out how to give myself the gift again the next night and the night after. My entire outlook on life felt different, and I attributed that to exercising the discipline to go to bed early and ignore the distractions of undone tasks or mindless phone use. The result was a simple feeling of clarity.

The research on sleep explains this feeling. "A good night's rest may literally clear the mind," according to the National Institutes of Health.[2] Their studies show that the space between brain cells may increase during sleep in order to flush out toxins that build up while we are awake. So sleep cleans up the brain, so to speak. That feeling of clarity after a full night's sleep is more than a feeling. Research also shows that sleep acts as a daily reset button that clears out stressors from the previous day.[3] It also helps us retain information we've learned, heals the damage done by stress, and empowers us to perform better on tests and tasks.

Sleep is so basic that it can be easy to crowd it out when we are short on time. But maybe, just maybe, this needs to be a nonnegotiable. As I drove to work that morning feeling so refreshed, I pondered the possibility of a splurge—nine hours of sleep per night for a full week. How might that change my outlook? My stress level? My ability to focus? So that was the experiment: nine-plus hours of sleep for seven nights. My weeklong quest to get better sleep left me feeling like a brand-new woman. I was more relaxed. My head felt clear rather than groggy when I woke up each morning. And what I noticed most was my mood. I had an extra reserve of energy and positive emotions throughout the day, did not get frustrated as easily, and stayed focused for longer periods of time.

Try your own sleep-reset experiment. For at least three consecutive days or more, commit to the following:

- Go to bed at the same time each night.
- Wake up at the same time each morning, including on weekends.

- Remove all technology from your room, including laptops, cell phones, and the television (you can unplug it if removing it is too cumbersome).
- Finish your last meal at least two hours before bedtime, and do not drink any alcohol or caffeine.
- Sleep at least eight hours—nine hours if you can!

DIGITAL DIET EXPERIMENTS

CREATE SOME "PHONE SPACE"

If your phone were your significant other, you'd probably feel pretty smothered in the relationship. It's always there, always doing something to demand your attention, never giving you any time to yourself. You might not be ready to break off the relationship, but you definitely might need to ask for some space. Yep. *Phone space.* We all need it. So here's your experiment: for the next three days, create some space between you and your phone by keeping your phone somewhere that requires you to get up or walk across a room to get it. Even if you are traveling, this experiment would mean you keep your phone inside a travel bag or purse instead of your pocket or hand.

The biggest time drain for a large number of people is time spent mindlessly using their phones. Even as far back as 2007, 91 percent of adults kept their phones within arm's reach at all times, according to a study by Morgan Stanley.[4] So an effective way to break a phone addiction is to disrupt the ease with which you are able to grab your phone as soon as you have the urge.

APP REVIEW

Look at all of the apps on your phone and honestly answer this question: What's your biggest time drain? A time drain is the ultimate screen seduction, tempting you to waste time on something that feels urgent but holds little or no meaning. This could be games, social media apps, shopping sites, news apps, real estate apps, or anything else that fits the description. Once you identify your time-sucking apps, delete them for a specific period of time—a month or a week, for example. Then notice how doing so impacts your time.

TECH-FREE CHALLENGE

Set up a "device drop box" by the front door or elsewhere away from the action, and for a period of time you and other household members surrender your mobile devices to the box and focus on conversation, activities, or quiet time without distraction. Create a consequence for anyone who succumbs to temptation, like they get to clear the table and do the dishes. Ideal tech-free times include meal times, gatherings, and early evenings after arriving home.

You can also come up with variations on tech-free experiments. For example, identify your most productive time of the day—perhaps the last two hours of your workday or the first hour you wake up—and commit to turning off your phone or disconnecting from Wi-Fi at that time.

SOCIAL MEDIA DETOX

If you are on social media daily and often feel you can't resist the urge, a social media detox can be a healthy experiment. Stop using it altogether for a period of time and then decide what would be healthy: A weekly check-in? Once a day for ten minutes? No more social media?

RELATIONSHIP EXPERIMENTS

THE CRUCIAL CONNECTION

Who in your life do you want to stay connected with but just don't see as often as you would like? You might text and talk, but you don't engage much face-to-face. Your crucial connections are just one or two people with whom you have a bond that you want to strengthen and maintain. Perhaps it is a parent, a sibling, or an important friend. Pick a frequency and period of time to get together—like lunch once a week on Fridays, breakfast once a month on the first Saturday, or a video chat every Thursday night. Schedule dates for the next month or two, and experiment with making a consistent, heartfelt connection.

ONE MEANINGFUL THING

Every morning for a week, declare One Meaningful Thing you will do that day, and construct the day around making it happen. For example, if you have a major project but struggle with procrastination, your One Meaningful Thing might be getting home in time for dinner with family or meeting a friend for an evening workout. By declaring your One Meaningful Thing, you intensify your focus on the work at hand and ensure you won't miss the important time with people who matter. Having something nonnegotiable that marks your day helps you focus on meaning and keeps you from getting overwhelmed by your tasks.

THE SLOW THANK-YOU

Instead of texting, write a heartfelt, handwritten thank-you note and snail-mail it. Writing a note slows you down and creates a treasure that can be tucked away and revisited over and over. Say the things you'd want the recipient to know if you were long gone. Make it meaningful. It'll take you five minutes.

REINSTATE THE DINNERTIME RITUAL

"Dinner time" used to be a thing. In many households, you didn't answer calls. Everybody sat down together around the table. You turned off the TV. You ate food cooked at home. According to Gallup, just over half of adults with children under eighteen eat dinner together most nights.[5] If you're in the half that doesn't, consider a dinnertime experiment—everyone eats together at the table, with no mobile devices or television, and just enjoys each other's company and conversation. Even if you're single, dinnertime can be a time to stop and reflect. Use your nice dishes, savor your meal, and relax.

ORGANIZATIONAL EXPERIMENTS

CREATE A "NOT TO DO" LIST

Everything on your to-do list falls under one of four categories: do it, delay it, delete it, or delegate it. The "Not to Do" list is all about deleting. Some things just don't need to be done. Drop it. Let it go. Free yourself. This can be fun. To-do lists can be helpful, but not everything on yours needs to be there. Grab your to-do list and make a "Not to Do" list by running each item on your list through these questions: Is this meaningful? Is it necessary? Does it need to happen now? As you start asking, "Do I have to have this lunch meeting? Do I need to get my haircut today? Do I need to go shopping for shoes today?" you may discover you're stressed by a demanding list that you could shorten by adjusting your expectations.

"YOU DO" LIST

This is one of my favorites. Take a look at your to-do list and pick everything on it that you can transfer to a "You Do" list, which is all about delegating. The task still gets done—it's just that *you* aren't the one who has to do it. Perhaps the kids, your spouse, someone else on the committee or team, or maybe the person who was supposed to do it in the first place can do it.

There are sometimes emotional struggles with the "You Do" list. You might feel guilty, like I did when my husband wisely suggested that our oldest two kids start doing their own laundry. Having grown up in a household where Mom did all the laundry, I somehow had this belief that that was how it was supposed to be. But with five people in the family, I was getting overwhelmed. Turning laundry into a "You Do" has been awesome indeed.

Sometimes it's not guilt but anxiety you feel when you turn tasks over to others. You can do it better. They might screw things up. Both might be true, and that's okay. Let them learn so the pressure is not all on you. Besides, some tasks are just not so meaningful that you should be the only one doing them. I mean, sure, maybe you fold the towels better than your eight-year-old, but they're just going to be taken right back out of the linen closet anyway, so does it really matter how well they're folded? I know, I know. If you are a neat freak, that statement sounds ridiculous. That used to be me, and I finally had to make a choice: meaningful or false urgency?

TIME YOUR TO-DO LIST

While we are on the subject of to-do lists, the main problem with them is this: there's too much on them! Tidsoptimism kicks in big-time on to-do lists, and most of the time what you've crammed into your list for a day's activities is simply impossible to accomplish for the number of hours there are in a day. For the next week, try "timing" your to-do list. Next to each item, use defensive pessimism to estimate the amount of time the task will take. Include prep time, phone calls, drive time, research, or anything else that will be needed to carry out the task. Add it up and compare it to how much time you actually have. What can you learn from what you see?

THE SAME-CHOICE EXPERIMENT

Remember that a culprit of time poverty is bandwidth. The more decisions you have to make, the more time poor you'll feel as even small decisions begin to feel cumbersome. The same-choice experiment allows you to make a choice about a repetitive decision so that you only have to make the decision once. For example, you can decide on the same thing for lunch every day this week—or the same item from a menu at your favorite restaurant. Or a seven-day rotation of dinner meals that repeats for a month. Apple founder Steve Jobs was known for his collection of black turtlenecks and jeans. That was his uniform, so to speak, and he didn't have to waste mental energy deciding what to wear. This can be done for hairstyles, food, clothing, even responses to repetitive requests. What same choice could you experiment with?

ACTION PLAN

The fun thing about experiments is you can make them your own. You can identify what you need and come up with ideas to experiment with. See overwhelming days when it seems you just don't have enough time as an opportunity to try out new ways of responding.

But how do you know what types of experiments to undertake or create? That requires getting to the heart of the problem you are currently facing and determining what your short-term and long-term needs are in relation to that. In essence, by asking yourself some direct questions and providing honest answers, you can develop an action plan that will help you consistently and purposefully implement the change you desire.

To coach yourself to a practical action plan, there are four steps:

1. Identify your goal.
2. Understand the obstacles.
3. Explore your options.
4. Commit to an action step.

For each of your long- and short-term goals, answer these coaching questions:

1. Short-term goal: Relieve the immediate pressure and clarify what's meaningful.

#MEANINGFULOVERURGENT

- What is the time demand that's overwhelming me right now?
- What vulnerabilities and realities have contributed to creating this problem?
- Is this problem a false urgency or is it meaningful?
- What experiments can I try that will support my vision? After trying the experiments:
  - Which changes will I keep and move forward with?
  - Which experiments will now become permanent fixtures?

2. Long-term goal: Bring your vision to fruition.
   - What are my key markers?
   - What will I need to do differently to get to my vision?
   - What steps can I take to lay the groundwork for my vision, and what is my timeline?
   - What experiments can I try that will support my vision? After trying the experiments:
     - Which changes will I keep and move forward with?
     - Which experiments will now become permanent fixtures?

SMALL SHIFTS CLARIFY YOUR BIG SHIFT

When I began this journey, I thought I knew exactly what it would look like to take control of my time: Less work. Less responsibility. Less of everything. My belief was that the only way to make space was to eliminate things in my life that take up time. But here's the power of experiments. As I took control of my time in little ways, I found clarity, and suddenly I had an aha moment about my belief: This was not my season to shrink my life. It was my season to expand. My goal was to have *more* impact, not less. So the answer was to change my approach. My life and business had grown significantly, but my approach had not. I had unrealistic expectations about how much I could accomplish personally. I needed to ask for help in key areas, let go of my expectations about what I could personally be responsible for, and say no a whole lot more. Use experiments to create small shifts, and you lay the foundation for big shifts.

. . . .

MEANINGFUL MINUTE

Action builds momentum. What's the first experiment you'd feel excited to try in order to take better control of your time and happiness?

_____

_____

_____

_____

CHAPTER TWELVE

BEST BUDGET EVER

If you are time poor, how do you climb out of time debt and build time wealth and happiness? Much like digging out of financial debt and building financial wealth, you need to become clear about where you are.

I'll never forget when I first decided I wanted to get out of financial debt in my twenties. I bought a book about finances, and it told me to add up all of my debt and savings and then track my spending for a week. I closed the book and put it on my bookshelf. Not only did I not want to know how much debt I had, but the idea of tracking my spending seemed cumbersome and tedious. I wanted out of debt, but I didn't want to do the work to get there. So I went about my life, continued to rack up debt, and chose denial over the truth by insisting things were not that bad because I had good credit and paid my bills on time. Never mind that I was stressed and stretched financially, didn't earn what I was worth, and lacked a cushion for emergencies.

The truth is, this is exactly how too many of us live when it comes to time debt and time poverty today. At least, that's how I was living.

It's time to pull together everything we've talked about on our journey through these pages and create a practical and inspiring plan of action. It begins with telling the truth about how you spend your time now, even if it's not the way you want to spend your time in the future. In other words, you need to become clear about where you are, in much the same way that I had to become clear years ago about my debt. Numbers are concrete. Once you see them, the stark reality can jolt you. And sometimes what we need most is a good jolt.

For example, as I mentioned earlier, the average person spends almost an hour per day on social media now. When you only consider that time as a proportion of one day, it may not seem terribly bad. However, if you consider it in the context of a whole month, you suddenly realize the average person is spending thirty-plus hours per month on social media. That's 360 hours a year! If you were suddenly given an extra 360 hours to use in a fulfilling way, what would you do? Even if you gave yourself half of that time back, what meaningful thing might you do with 180 hours? Take more naps? Lose the extra twenty pounds you'd like to shed? Spend time with people you love? Start the business or write the book you've dreamed of?

Your possibilities for building a more meaningful life and letting go of the false urgency of time stealers that have become habit are abundant. It begins with clarifying exactly where you are right now when it comes to how you spend your time.

TRANSFORM YOUR TIME CHART INTO A TIME BUDGET

As you've seen, creating a time chart can be an eye-opening experience. But how do you apply the data you've collected and translate it into real-life change? Consider Jamie, the mother who snapped at her daughter when she asked what's for dinner. Her time chart before making changes looked like this:

Daily Time Chart

TIME EXPENSE	ESTIMATED AMOUNT OF TIME SPENT IN HOURS	PERCENT OF TIME USED (BASED ON 24-HOUR DAY)
Sleeping	7	29
Eating	1.5	6
Preparing for meals	0.5	2
Commuting	1.3	5
Exercising	0	0
Working	8	33
Traveling for work (not commuting)	0	0
Getting kids ready for school/bed	0.5	2
Doing homework (yours or your children's)	0.5	2
Attending school	0	0
Spending time as a household	0.5	2
Maintaining personal hygiene	0.5	2
Engaging in leisure time	0	0
Driving family members/friends	0.5	2
Grocery shopping	0.5	2
Doing laundry	0.25	1
Cleaning the house	0.25	1
Socializing with friends	0.5	2
Browsing social media	0.5	2

Watching television/other screen viewing (includes internet time other than social media)	0.5	2
Attending hair/nail appointments	0	0
Engaging in self-care activities	0	0
Participating in extracurricular activities (yours or your children's)	0.5	2
Attending health appointments	0	0
Dating/romantic activities	0	0
Spending time with extended family	0	0
Worshiping	0	0

Total daily hours expended: 23.8

Balance: 0.2

Percent of time spent (daily hours expended divided by 24): 99

Weekly Time Chart

TIME EXPENSE	ESTIMATED AMOUNT OF TIME SPENT IN HOURS	PERCENT OF TIME USED (BASED ON 168-HOUR WEEK)
Sleeping	45.5	27
Eating	10.5	6
Preparing for meals	11.5	7

Commuting	6.5	4
Exercising	0	0
Working	40	24
Working overtime	2	1
Traveling for work (not commuting)	0	0
Getting kids ready for school/bed	3.5	2
Doing homework (yours or your children's)	2.5	1
Attending school	0	0
Spending time as a household	5	3
Maintaining personal hygiene	7	4
Engaging in leisure time	1	1
Driving family members/friends	3.5	2
Grocery shopping	2.5	1
Doing laundry	2.5	1
Cleaning the house	3	2
Socializing with friends	2	1
Browsing social media	11	7
Watching television/other screen viewing (includes internet time other than social media)	4	2
Attending hair/nail appointments	1.5	1
Engaging in self-care activities	2	1

Participating in extracurricular activities (yours or your children's)	5	3
Attending health appointments	0	0
Dating/romantic activities	1	1
Spending time with extended family	0	0
Worshiping	2	1
Volunteering	1	1
Spending time on a hobby	0	0

Total weekly hours expended: 176
Balance: -8
Percent of time spent (weekly hours expended divided by 168): 105

Although Jamie felt stressed and regularly complained about not having enough time in the day, seeing that she was running a deficit of more than eight hours per week was sobering. And she realized that more and more, she was borrowing time from the future. She had cut into her sleep time and stopped exercising. She and her husband rarely had much time alone, let alone time for dates and fun. She had cut out some of the most important and meaningful aspects of her life just to keep up, and she still fell short on time. She knew some changes were needed and some tough choices had to be made. Making the time chart gave her the information she needed to see her time demands clearly, which allowed her to wisely make choices about what was meaningful versus what might be merely a false urgency at this point in her life.

Take a look at the time chart you created when you began this journey. Then ask two questions:

- What looming projects or activities do I need to attend to but have put off?
- What would I like to be able to use my time to do that I am currently not doing?

These two questions represent your time debt. Include the things you want to be able to do but don't currently have time for. This is a critical step because it is the only way to get an honest and accurate picture of your time debt and begin setting up a time budget of your ideal scenario.

Just as a financial budget helps you decide how you want your money to be spent, a time budget helps you decide how you want your time to be spent. It helps you intentionally choose what is meaningful for you. The art of choosing the meaningful over the urgent becomes easier when you look at the numbers. It will naturally spark some self-reflection. Pay attention to the powerful questions that emerge.

- When I look at my time chart, what bothers me? Is there an activity or a glaring problem that jolts me?
- What is in my vision that is not currently in my time chart?
- What elements of my vision could I budget?
- What key markers would I like to incorporate into my time budget? Remember, "key markers" are things that let you know you are using your time meaningfully, such as my key marker of nightly sunset-watching.

The purpose of creating your time budget is to:

- Establish how much time you want to allocate to each of your time expenses. This may differ from the time you are currently spending in each category. In your time budget, you are saying, "This is the goal. This is what I am aiming to do." In contrast, your time chart is saying, "This is what I am currently doing."

- Identify categories where you can save time, and make decisions about how you will save time.
- Evaluate whether your time expenses reflect four categories of time expenses: spending, saving, giving, and investing. Let's talk more about these four categories.

SPENDING TIME

Just as with money, building time wealth is about using your time in ways that are healthy, fulfilling, and prosperous. If you save all of your time, you won't be productive. Spending is both healthy and productive, but you want to spend in the right ways. The spending category of your time budget is where you declare what gets your time. Keep in mind that around 60 percent of your time is likely already accounted for just by eating, sleeping, and working. Eating averages ten to fifteen hours per week for most people. With a goal of the recommended eight hours per night, sleep adds up to fifty-six hours per week. If you work outside the home forty hours per week and have a commute of thirty minutes each way, work takes about forty-five hours per week. Even if you don't work outside the home, it is likely you spend twenty hours or more on other types of work, which means nearly half of your hours are still taken up by these three categories. Your goal in determining what you will spend your remaining time on is to align your time with your vision—the meaningful priorities you identified earlier in our journey.

Just as you have fixed expenses in your financial budget—things such as rent or a mortgage, utilities, and groceries—you have fixed time expenses. Fixed time expenses are those things that, in this season of life, you must do no matter what. Your fixed time might include working, child care, sleep, and eating. In a different season of life, some fixed time expenses might change. For example, your baby will grow up, and child care will no longer be a fixed expense on your time budget. You might retire or accumulate enough money that you can work less or not at all. However, some fixed time expenses are just a fact of life—sleeping and eating; for example.

Discretionary time is the time you have available to do whatever you like. This can include socializing, hobbies, education, volunteering, and anything else at your discretion. These are the activities that best express your values and priorities. You can always look at a person's discretionary time to determine what is important to them and what makes them tick.

Ask yourself these PQs to help you *spend* your time more meaningfully:

TIME-SPENDING PQS

- Am I pleased with how much time I am spending in each category in this season of my life?
- What might I change, if anything? Why is it meaningful to change it?
- What false urgencies do I see?
- What elements of my vision are not currently reflected in my time chart? What elements of my vision could I incorporate into my time budget?
- When I have extra discretionary time, what priorities do I want to spend it on?

For every item you add to your time budget, you must do two things: (1) use the skill of positive pessimism to reasonably estimate the time needed, and (2) determine where the time will come from to add the activity. If your time chart indicates you have plenty of discretionary time, this is easy. But if you don't have the discretionary time, you'll need to figure out where you can save time.

SAVING TIME

Wasting time is as easy as wasting money, probably easier. After all, you are *always* spending time, though you are not always spending money. Even if you don't want to spend time, you are. There is no stopping the clock; it ticks relentlessly. So saving time differs dramatically from the concept of saving money, which you can literally stockpile, put to the side, and pull out later to use when you are ready. Therefore, the act of saving time must be an intentional choice. To save time is to look at ways you may be inefficient, make adjustments, and then intentionally allocate the saved time to a spending, giving, or investing category that is more meaningful for you.

There are five basic ways to save time:

- **Delete.** Not everything you are doing is meaningful or necessary. Sometimes a task or commitment was meaningful or necessary in a different season of your life, but now it's time to let it go.
- **Delay.** Some things are simply not necessary right now. Perhaps you don't have the necessary information to complete the task. Maybe you don't have the time, and there would be little consequence to moving it to a later date. Or perhaps you can divide the task into smaller steps and take a step now while spacing out the other steps over a period of time.
- **Delegate.** Look at every item on your time chart to determine what could be done by someone else. Delegating immediately frees up some time.
- **Duplicate.** If you think ahead, there are often ways to double

up so that you accomplish two goals simultaneously. You can exercise with a friend, or listen to an audiobook or catch up on calls (hands-free, if you're driving) during your commute.

- **Discover.** Sometimes you don't know what you don't know—and that means it's time to investigate ways to do things differently. Be open to new ideas. Talk to others in your circumstances or those who've "been there, done that." Look for ways to save time, and you are likely to find them.

For example, if we look at Jamie's time chart, we can see that she is currently in time debt eight hours per week. Even so, she's not exercising at all, and she is only getting six and a half hours of sleep. So before she can add anything, she must first prune her time by finding places she can decrease or cut time expenses altogether. Work and commuting are not flexible right now, nor is homework time. But Jamie wants to find time to exercise, and as you may remember, her family admittedly gets the short end of the stick. Her husband has started complaining about their lack of quality time, her parents are only twenty minutes away but don't see her often, and the kids complain she's always preoccupied with her phone. What would you do if you were Jamie?

The first thing it makes sense to do is look at her time chart and ask a set of powerful questions. This is the same approach you should take to create workable solutions for your own time budget. Ask these PQs to help you *save* time intentionally.

TIME-SAVING PQS

- Are there time expenses I can cut or eliminate? How? When?
- What do I see on my time chart that I can delegate?
- What discretionary time expenses can be put on hold until I get a better handle on my schedule?
- What time expenses could I combine and do simultaneously?

- What am I spending time on that is a lower priority than something I want to spend time on?
- What are the priorities that will get my "saved time"?

In evaluating her time expenses, Jamie found several areas in which she could save time, reduce her time debt, and better align her time budget with her priorities. She used the tools of deleting, delegating, and duplicating to free up some time. For example, she had a weekly "Wine Wind Down" on Fridays with her girlfriends, but no regular date night with her husband. She decided to delete the girlfriend get-together every other Friday and have a date night with her husband on alternating Fridays. While this did not reduce her time debt, it created space for more time with her husband.

She was also spending way too much time on social media, and she knew it. Deep down, she hated to admit it felt like an addiction sometimes, but it seemed to soothe her stress (even though it multiplied her guilt because it caused her to procrastinate and at times ignore the people in her life). Because she logged on throughout the day and then scrolled mindlessly while lying in bed at night, saying it helped her wind down, she estimated it consumed at least an hour and a half per day. She committed to cutting that to thirty minutes per day and leaving her phone charging by the front door overnight. That way she wouldn't be tempted. This decision gave her an extra seven hours per week—nearly erasing her eight-hour weekly time debt.

As you may remember, she delegated dinner to her two oldest children twice per week, which freed up another hour and fully eliminated her time debt.

But Jamie didn't want to have just enough time; she wanted time for priorities she'd neglected and some extra discretionary time to spend as she pleased. So she decided to find time for exercise—four days per week for thirty minutes—and two hours of extra discretionary time. That meant she needed to find a way to save four more hours. She combed her time chart to look for more savings opportunities and pondered the following question: What was on her time chart that she resisted changing even though it would be wise to do so?

She had two inklings that were authentic answers to the question. She hated to admit it, but the Friday nights with her friends had become a gossip-and-complaint session, and there was really only one friend in the group she enjoyed, and that friend lived just five minutes away. So she dropped the "Wine Wind Down" entirely, letting the group know that she was making some changes to her schedule and life, and would need to be with her family on Fridays. They all understood. Second, deep down, she sensed that thirty minutes a day on social media was still a waste. She found herself feeling worse after scrolling, not better—comparing her life to others, feeling anxious about how many likes and comments her posts were getting. It felt silly, but it was the truth.

She decided to duplicate her time. She invited her friend to take a thirty-minute walk with her a couple of times a week so they could chat and catch up. Both of them had been talking about getting back into an exercise routine. To make time for that, Jamie decided to cut her social media time even further—a max of three times per week for up to thirty minutes. That freed up thirty minutes four times per week.

As you look at your time chart, ask yourself the Time-Saving PQs to help uncover opportunities to save time so you can align your priorities with your actual schedule.

GIVING TIME

Giving time includes time helping others in some way, whether by being a listening ear, giving advice over the phone or in person, showing up to be supportive, or volunteering. Spending and saving time are fundamental, but giving time is just plain fun. Giving time is about intentionally giving of yourself to the people and causes that matter most to you.

Nothing boosts your happiness like serving others. When our time is only about us and what we want, there is something missing. Your time is valuable to other people, whether it's your spouse and children, parents and siblings, significant other, friends, extended family, coworkers, neighbors, and even those you don't know who are in need.

Your time is most valuable in those roles in your life that are irreplaceable. If you are married, no one else can replace your role as a spouse. You are the only spouse your spouse has. If you are a mother, you are the only mother your child has. You cannot be replaced; therefore, consider the impact your time has because no one else can fill your shoes. That role on the committee? Someone else can do that job if needed. Keep that in mind when making difficult choices about where to give your time, especially when your time is limited.

Ask these powerful questions to help you give your time purposefully.

TIME-GIVING PQS

- Whom do I want to impact? How?
- What can I do that is meaningful and takes little time?
- What do I want to do that is meaningful and may take more time?
- How much discretionary time do I want to allocate to giving?
- If I do not have discretionary time in my time chart right now, where will I find it?

INVESTING TIME

The last, and perhaps most powerful, category of your time budget is investing. In a financial budget, the goal of investing is to reap a return at a later date so that you can meet financial needs or wants you may have in the future. There is typically no expectation of an immediate return on an investment. This is the case with investing your time as well.

Looking at your current time chart, with the fixed time expenses that are a necessity right now, you may be unable to see how you will ever escape time poverty and build time wealth. It may look as though you'll always be time poor because you can only figure out how to save an hour or two here or there. But if you begin investing your time now, your life in the future can be exactly as you dream.

Investing your time, though, is about putting yourself in a position to bring your full vision to fruition. It might include choosing a new career path or pursing opportunities that help you meet future goals. Perhaps it includes looking for opportunities that generate passive income so that time is no longer your only option for making money. It could include setting yourself up financially so you don't have to work at all. It may include a move to a city near family where you'll have more support and a strong social network. It might include marriage or having independent adult children who can leave the nest and make it successfully on their own, allowing you to enjoy an empty nest free of worry. Ask yourself these time-investing PQs to get clarity:

TIME-INVESTING PQS

- What are some long-term goals I should spend time working toward now?
- What will these goals give me that I don't have right now?

- What can I do consistently that will move me effectively toward this vision?

This part of your time budget is the easiest to skip—and the most detrimental if you do. You'll be tempted to blow it off and insist you'll get to it later. But when later comes, I promise you'll regret not having more love for your future self. Make a decision to invest your time in creating the future you have dreamed of.

YOUR TIME BUDGET

Now let's see what your time budget looks like. This is your road map, rooted in all that we've learned on this journey. (Visit valorieburton. com for downloadable versions.)

Daily Time Budget

TIME EXPENSE	ESTIMATED AMOUNT OF TIME SPENT IN HOURS	PERCENT OF TIME USED (BASED ON 24-HOUR DAY)
Sleeping		
Eating		
Preparing for meals		
Commuting		
Exercising		
Working		
Traveling for work (not commuting)		

Getting kids ready for school/bed		
Doing homework (yours or your children's)		
Attending school		
Spending time as a household		
Maintaining personal hygiene		
Engaging in leisure time		
Driving family members/friends		
Grocery shopping		
Doing laundry		
Cleaning the house		
Socializing with friends		
Browsing social media		
Watching television/other screen viewing (includes internet time other than social media)		
Attending hair/nail appointments		
Engaging in self-care activities		
Participating in extracurricular activities (yours or your children's)		
Attending health appointments		

Dating/romantic activities		
Spending time with extended family		
Worshiping		

Total daily hours expended: _____

Balance: _____

Percent of time spent (daily hours expended divided by 24): _____

Weekly Time Budget

TIME EXPENSE	ESTIMATED AMOUNT OF TIME SPENT IN HOURS	PERCENT OF TIME USED (BASED ON 168-HOUR WEEK)
Sleeping		
Eating		
Preparing for meals		
Commuting		
Exercising		
Working		
Traveling for work (not commuting)		

Getting kids ready for school/bed		
Doing homework (yours or your children's)		
Attending school		
Spending time as a household		
Maintaining personal hygiene		
Engaging in leisure time		
Driving family members/friends		
Grocery shopping		
Doing laundry		
Cleaning the house		
Socializing with friends		
Browsing social media		
Watching television/other screen viewing (includes internet time other than social media)		
Attending hair/nail appointments		
Engaging in self-care activities		
Participating in extracurricular activities (yours or your children's)		
Attending health appointments		

Dating/romantic activities		
Spending time with extended family		
Worshiping		

Total weekly hours expended: _____

Balance: _____

Percent of time spent (weekly hours expended divided by 168): _____

· ·

Monthly Time Budget

TIME EXPENSE	ESTIMATED AMOUNT OF TIME SPENT IN HOURS	PERCENT OF TIME USED (BASED ON 720-HOUR MONTH)
Sleeping		
Eating		
Preparing for meals		
Commuting		
Exercising		
Working		
Traveling for work (not commuting)		

Getting kids ready for school/bed		
Doing homework (yours or your children's)		
Attending school		
Spending time as a household		
Maintaining personal hygiene		
Engaging in leisure time		
Driving family members/friends		
Grocery shopping		
Doing laundry		
Cleaning the house		
Socializing with friends		
Browsing social media		
Watching television/other screen viewing (includes internet time other than social media)		
Attending hair/nail appointments		
Engaging in self-care activities		
Participating in extracurricular activities (yours or your children's)		
Attending health appointments		

Dating/romantic activities		
Spending time with extended family		
Worshiping		

Total monthly hours expended: _____

Balance: _____

Percent of time spent (monthly hours expended divided by 720): _____

Use your time budget as a guide. Revise it as you learn and grow. It is a tool. You can also complete your time budget online at www.valorieburton.com.

Just like any budget, your time budget is not to be looked at once and then tucked away. This needs to become a living document. As you seek to live by it, give yourself permission to stumble a bit, especially at first, but don't give up. Lasting change requires us to keep at it, to fall and get back up, over and over. The reward is a life in which time is not a relentless, demanding tyrant but a generous companion that graces you with the precious gift of true happiness.

CONCLUSION

J ust before sunset, Alex followed me to the garden. The cabbage, brussels sprouts, and tomato plants had taken root. The leaves were getting big. And we could see buds sprouting up where we had planted seeds for carrots, broccoli, and squash.

I was pulling tiny weeds when Alex excitedly yelled, "Look! Mommy! Look!" I stopped and looked up, fully expecting him to tell me he'd found a new stick in the yard that he was sure was a ninja sword he could use to fight "monster trees" behind the house. Instead, I saw him squatting in front of a plant at the edge of the garden. "It's a vegetable!" he squealed in awe.

Indeed, it was. Maybe two inches long, plump, and nestled beneath a bundle of sprouting leaves was a deep-green bell pepper. Our first vegetable! I was excited.

Growing a garden takes a vision. You decide what you want in your garden. You find a spot where the sun will shine. You till the soil and feed it with nutrients. You sow the seeds. Then every day you care for it. You weed it. You keep the pests away. No matter how much time you put in on a given day, you can't make things grow any faster. It is the consistency of daily nurturing that eventually yields a harvest.

The same is true of our relationship with time. If you consciously make the right choices, day after day, the vision will come to fruition. As I look at the harvest that continues to unfold in my life since beginning the journey out of time poverty, I am as much in awe as Alex was that day in the garden.

My garden has yielded much fruit: a calmer spirit, a home that reflects our dreams, a stronger partnership with my husband, memorable trips with extended family, intentional memories with our children, a more enjoyable workload, more breathing room, more fun, more meaning, more sunsets. I have learned to say no more easily and yes more enthusiastically.

I have learned many lessons along the way, lessons I have shared in these pages. The ones I hope you and I will never forget are these:

- Stop treating things as equally important when they're not. With so many options and time demands, it is easy to lose sight of what really matters.
- It's okay to miss out. Not every season of your life is meant for every experience. Be courageous enough to let go so you can make room for what's meaningful in this season.
- If you don't value your time, you will spend it on people and things that are not worthy of it. Refuse to allow your insecurities and vulnerabilities to make choices for you about how to spend your time.
- The modern world tells us that time is valuable because time is money. This is a myth. Time is valuable because, unlike money, it cannot be replaced.
- Know when you've done enough. More is not always better.
- What is meaningful is *timeless*. It matters today. It matters in the future. It shapes your legacy.

Like yours, my journey is a work in progress. When the weeds of distraction try to choke out the good habits I am building, I pause and use powerful questions, ask for help, or give myself a chance to simply choose again. In a world where what's become normal is simply not natural, we can make choices that bring meaning and happiness.

When you get stuck, come back to these pages. This is not a book to be read once and put on the shelf, but a guide and companion to equip you with the knowledge and tools to do what matters. Revisit these pages as often as you need to. The inspiration to persevere to your vision will be right here. It's about time you have a life that reflects the happiness that comes from choosing the meaningful over the urgent.

Love and Blessings,

Valorie Burton

ACKNOWLEDGMENTS

This book exists because of the support of devoted, gifted people in my life. I did not do this alone. Not even close. I especially want to thank the following:

My amazing husband, Jeff. Your willingness to jump into this journey with me not only made it fun but has transformed how we think about and spend our time. Thank you for your wholehearted commitment to me, to our dreams, and to helping me write the book we both needed.

Sophie, Addie, and Alex, our children. The journey with you makes my life so much more meaningful. You are what this book is about—making time, making memories, and making choices that create a meaningful legacy. Thank you for being you.

Daisy Hutton, you rock. Thank you for inviting me to join the W family. Your vision and guidance have blown me away. You stretched me in ways I wanted to be stretched, and I am better for it. Thank you for passionately embracing this book and providing the road map to help me write it.

Andrea Heinecke, my literary agent. You believed more was possible even when I couldn't see it. Thank you for encouraging and supporting me every step of the way.

Yvette Cook, my phenomenal friend and COO of Inspire Inc. Your unwavering friendship, brainstorming sessions, personal stories, and ideas made this journey more meaningful and the book more powerful. You were there when the idea for this book became clear in the Phoenix airport that day, and you stuck by me every step of the way—reading chapters, letting me read passages out loud, helping me when it felt hard. I appreciate you so very much.

Kristin Tucker, my talented and beautiful godsister and personal editor. Working with you on this book was a heaven-sent gift! Thank you for the countless hours editing and talking concepts through. I could not have made it through that first big edit without you and your relentless focus. You are such a brilliant and disciplined writer and editor. You make it look effortless. I can't wait to see your book in print and your credits rolling on the big screen! Thank you for being there for me.

Meaghan Porter, senior editor at W Publishing. Thank you for making this manuscript better! I appreciate your ability to fine-tune and enhance the spirit of my message.

Denise George, Kristi Smith, Becky Melvin, and Ashley Reed—my marketing and publicity team at W Publishing. Thank you for your passion, creativity, and effort on this project! It is a joy to work with you.

Senia Maymin, PhD, my dear friend and colleague. Thank you for being a sounding board, coach, and true encourager. I admire and appreciate your excellence and humility.

Leone Murray, my mom. You have cheered me on from the day I embarked on my journey as a writer. Your support is so consistent and caring. From encouraging me when I feel stuck to babysitting when I need a few extra hours to meet a deadline—I don't even have to ask. You go ahead of me and make a way. Not to mention my passion for books is a gift from you. Thank you.

Johnny Burton, my dad. You've always encouraged me and said

that I could do absolutely anything. Your belief in me made me bold enough to believe I could pursue my dreams. And my love of communication is something I got from you. Thank you.

Wade and Alexis Murray, my brother and sister-in-love. Thank you for your enthusiasm, your love, and your hard work to help bring the vision for this book to life!

Natasha McCain, my hairstylist. Thanks for getting me ready for this cover shoot! You are fabulous at what you do!

Briana Jones, my make up artist for this cover shoot. Thank you for your warm spirit, excellent professionalism, and natural touch!

I am blessed with many family members, friends, and colleagues who have made this journey fun, meaningful, and life changing. You know who you are. Thank you for those conversations and interactions that kept me inspired and moving forward.

And to you, the reader. Thank you for the opportunity to share this message and the chance to help you transform your life.

NOTES

CHAPTER 1: THE NEW NORMAL IS *NOT NORMAL*

1. "ACA Facts and Trends," American Camp Association, accessed November 27, 2018, https://www.acacamps.org/press-room/aca-facts-trends.

2. Michael Yogman, Andrew Garner, Jeffrey Hutchinson, Kathy Hirsh-Pasek, and Roberta Michnick Golinkoff, "The Power of Play: A Pediatric Role in Enhancing Development in Young Children," *American Academy of Pediatrics* 142, no. 3 (September 2018).

3. "Media Use in School-Aged Children and Adolescents," American Academy of Pediatrics, October 2016, pediatrics.aappublications.org/content/early/2016/10/19/peds.2016-2592.

4. Tami Luhby, "Gen Xers Are Poorer Than Their Parents," CNN Money, September 22, 2014, https://money.cnn.com/2014/09/22/news/economy/gen-x-poorer-than-parents-pew-study/index.html.

5. Sarah O'Connor, "Stagnant Wages and Rising House Prices Hit Disposable Income Levels," *Financial Times*, February 23, 2018, https://www.ft.com/content/81343d9e-187b-11e8-9e9c-25c814761640.

6. John Ydstie, "The American Dream Is Harder to Find in Some Neighborhoods," NPR, *Morning Edition*, October 1, 2018, https://www.npr.org/2018/10/01/649701669/the-american-dream-is-harder-to-find-in-some-neighborhoods.

7. "37 Percent of May 2016 Employment in Occupations Typically Requiring Postsecondary Education," *The Economics Daily*, Bureau of Labor Statistics, June 28, 2017, https://www.bls.gov/opub/ted/2017/37-percent-of-may-2016-employment-in-occupations-typically-requiring-postsecondary-education.htm.

8. Abby Jackson, "It Was the Hardest Year on Record to Get into Elite Colleges—Admissions Experts Explain Why," *Business Insider*, December 20, 2017, https://www.businessinsider.com/former-ivy-league-admissions-directors-say-its-harder-than-ever-to-get-into-elite-schools-2016-11.

9. Maria Konnikova, "No Money, No Time," *New York Times*, June 13, 2014, https://opinionator.blogs.nytimes.com/2014/06/13/no-clocking-out/.

10. Konnikova, "No Money, No Time," *New York Times*.

11. Sendhil Mullainathan and Eldar Shafir, "Freeing Up Intelligence," *Scientific American Mind*, January/February 2014, https://scholar.harvard.edu/files/sendhil/files/scientificamericanmind0114-58.pdf.

CHAPTER 2: IS IT EVER ENOUGH?

1. David Cohen, "How Much Time Will the Average Person Spend on Social Media During Their Life?," *Adweek*, March 22, 2017, https://www.adweek.com/digital/mediakix-time-spent-social-media-infographic/.

2. "Welcome to the Happiest Country on Earth," CBS News, March 19, 2017, https://www.cbsnews.com/news/welcome-to-the-happiest-country-on-earth/.

3. Derek Thompson, "The Free-Time Paradox in America," *Atlantic*, September 13, 2016, https://www.theatlantic.com/business/archive/2016/09/the-free-time-paradox-in-america/499826/.

4. James Truslow Adams, *The Epic of America* (New York: Blue Ribbon Books, Inc., 1931), 404.

5. Adams, *The Epic of America*, 404.

CHAPTER 3: TIME POOR, TECH BLOATED

1. John Maynard Keynes, *Essays in Persuasion* (New York: W.W. Norton & Co., 1963), 358–73, http://www.econ.yale.edu/smith/econ116a/keynes1.pdf.

2. Corilyn Shropshire, "Americans Prefer Texting to Talking, Report Says," *Chicago Tribune*, March 26, 2015, http://www.chicagotribune.com/business/ct-americans-texting-00327-biz-20150326-story.html.

3. Adam Alter, *Irresistible: The Rise of Addictive Technology and the Business of Keeping Us Hooked* (New York: Penguin Press, 2017).

4. Edward Archer, Carl J. Lavie, Samantha M. McDonald, Diana M. Thomas, James R. Hébert, Sharon E. Taverno Ross, Kerry L. McIver, Robert M. Malina, Steven N. Blair, "Maternal Inactivity: 45-Year Trends in Mothers' Use of Time," *Mayo Clinic Proceedings* 88, no. 12 (December 2013): 1368–77.

5. Michele Corriston, "Woman Dies in Car Crash While Posting to Facebook About Pharrell's Song 'Happy,'" *People Magazine*, April 27, 2014, https://people.com/celebrity/woman-dies-in-car-crash-while-posting-to-facebook-about-pharrells-song-happy/.

6. Molly Soat, "Social Media Triggers a Dopamine High," American Marketing Association, November 2015, https://www.ama.org/publications/MarketingNews/Pages/feeding-the-addiction.aspx.

7. David Cohen, "How Much Time Will the Average Person Spend on Social Media During Their Life?," *Adweek*, March 22, 2017, https://www.adweek.com/digital/mediakix-time-spent-social-media-infographic/.

8. "Study: Young People More Inclined to Choose Social Media over Sex," CBS News, October 10, 2012, https://www.cbsnews.com/news/study-young-people-more-inclined-to-choose-social-media-over-sex/.

9. Roy F. Baumeister, Ellen Bratslavsky, Mark Muraven, and Dianne M. Tice, "Ego Depletion: Is the Active Self a Limited Resource?" *Journal of Personality and Social Psychology* 74, no. 5 (1998): 1252–65.

10. Nicholas G. Carr, *The Shallows: What the Internet Is Doing to Our Brains* (New York: W.W. Norton, 2010), 123–26.

11. Eyal Ophir, Clifford Nass, and Anthony D. Wagner, "Cognitive Control in Media Multitaskers," *Proceedings of the National Academy of Sciences*, August 24, 2009, http://www.pnas.org/content/106/37/15583; see also Adam Gorlick, "Media Multitaskers Pay Mental Price, Stanford Study Shows," *Stanford Report*, August 24, 2009, http://news

.stanford.edu/news/2009/august24/multitask-research-study
-082409.html.

12. Barbara L. Fredrickson, "Positive Emotions Broaden and Build," in
Patricia Devine and Ashby Plant, eds., *Advances in Experimental Social
Psychology*, vol. 47 (Burlington: Academic Press, 2013), 1–53.

13. Russell B. Clayton, Glenn Leshner, and Anthony Almond, "The
Extended iSelf: The Impact of iPhone Separation on Cognition,
Emotion, and Physiology," *Journal of Computer-Mediated
Communication* 20, no. 2 (January 8, 2015), https://onlinelibrary
.wiley.com/doi/epdf/10.1111/jcc4.12109.

CHAPTER 4: THE BIG BOOM

1. "1800 Census," accessed October 1, 2018, https://web.archive.org
/web/20070127110235/http://www.1930census.com/1800_census
.php; "1800 United States Census," accessed October 1, 2018, https://
en.wikipedia.org/wiki/1800_United_States_Census; "World Population
Growth," first published 2013, updated April 2017, accessed October 1,
2018, https://ourworldindata.org/world-population-growth.

2. "Why Do We Have Time Zones?," accessed October 1, 2018, https://
www.timeanddate.com/time/time-zones-history.html.

3. "1900 United States Census," accessed October 1, 2018, https://
en.wikipedia.org/wiki/1900_United_States_Census; "World
Population," accessed October 1, 2018, https://en.wikipedia.org/wiki
/World_population.

4. Edward E. Baptist, *The Half Has Never Been Told: Slavery and the
Making of American Capitalism* (New York: Basic Books, 2016).

5. "Why Do We Have Time Zones?," accessed October 1, 2018.

6. "U.S. Population in Millions: 1940 to 2050," U.S. Census Bureau,
1940 to 2010 Decennial Censuses, 2008 National Population
Projections, accessed November 27, 2018, https://www.census.gov
/newsroom/cspan/1940census/CSPAN_1940slides.pdf; "World
Population," accessed October 1, 2018, https://en.wikipedia.org/wiki
/World_population.

7. "List of Most Populous Cities in the United States by Decade,"

accessed October 1, 2018, https://en.wikipedia.org/wiki/List_of
_most_populous_cities_in_the_United_States_by_decade.

8. Mark A. Stevens, *Merriam-Webster's Collegiate Encyclopedia* (2000), s.v.
"Ford Model T 1927."

9. Keith Reid, "Happy Days—For Petroleum Marketers, the 1950s Lived
Up to the Nostalgia," *National Petroleum News* (June 2004): 24–25.

CHAPTER 5: HOW CHANGING TIMES HAVE CHANGED OUR TIME

1. John Helliwell, Richard Layard, and Jeffrey Sachs, *World Happiness
Report*, accessed November 27, 2018, http://www.earth.columbia.edu
/sitefiles/file/Sachs%20Writing/2012/World%20Happiness%20
Report.pdf.

2. Lisa C. Walsh, Julia K. Boehm, and Sonja Lyubomirsky, "Does
Happiness Promote Career Success? Revisiting the Evidence," *Journal
of Career Assessment* 26, no. 2 (2018): 199–219; see also Ed Diener,
Laura King, and Sonja Lyubomirsky, "The Benefits of Frequent
Positive Affect: Does Happiness Lead to Success?," *American
Psychological Association* 131, no. 6 (2005): 803–55.

3. Betsey Stevenson and Justin Wolfers, "The Paradox of Declining
Female Happiness," Institute for the Study of Labor (IZA), discussion
papers, 1 (2009): 10.1257/pol.1.2.190.

4. Stevenson and Wolfers, "The Paradox of Declining Female
Happiness."

5. Nolan Feeney, "Women Are Now More Likely to Have College
Degree Than Men," *Time*, October 7, 2015, http://time.com/4064665
/women-college-degree/; see also Hironao Okahana and Enyu Zhou,
Graduate Enrollment and Degrees: 2006 to 2016 (Washington, DC:
Council of Graduate Schools, 2017); "Chore Wars: Men, Women and
Housework," National Science Foundation, accessed October 1, 2018,
https://www.nsf.gov/discoveries/disc_images.jsp?cntn_id=111458.

6. "Employment Characteristics of Families Summary," Bureau of Labor
Statistics, April 19, 2018, https://www.bls.gov/news.release/famee.nr0.htm.

7. U.S. Census Bureau History: Public Broadcasting, accessed July 3,

2018, https://www.census.gov/history/www/homepage_archive/2015
/october_2015.html.

8. Ellen R. McGrattan and Richard Rogerson, "Changes in the
Distribution of Family Hours Worked Since 1950," *Federal Reserve
Bank of Minneapolis Research Department Staff Report* 397, revised
April 2008, retrieved November 18, 2018, https://www
.minneapolisfed.org/research/SR/SR397bw.pdf.

9. "Raising Kids and Running a Household: How Working Parents
Share the Load," Pew Research Center, November 4, 2015, accessed
July 3, 2018, http://www.pewsocialtrends.org/2015/11/04/raising-kids
-and-running-a-household-how-working-parents-share-the-load/.

10. "Raising Kids and Running a Household," Pew Research Center,
accessed July 3, 2018.

11. George Masnick, "The Rise of the Single-Person Household," Joint
Center for Housing Studies of Harvard University, May 20, 2015,
accessed July 3, 2018, http://www.jchs.harvard.edu/blog
/the-rise-of-the-single-person-household/.

12. Masnick, "The Rise of the Single-Person Household."

13. Stephanie Coontz, "Divorce, No-Fault Style," *New York Times*,
June 16, 2010, https://www.nytimes.com/2010/06/17/opinion
/17coontz.html.

14. "Will Social Security Save Retirement? Many Americans Think So,
According to New Personal Capital Survey," PR Newswire, accessed
November 27, 2018, https://www.prnewswire.com/news-releases
/will-social-security-save-retirement-many-americans-think-so
-according-to-new-personal-capital-survey-300672157.html.

15. "The First Mobile Phone Call Was Placed 40 Years Ago Today," Fox
News, November 5, 2015, accessed July 3, 2018, https://www.foxnews
.com/tech/the-first-mobile-phone-call-was-placed-40-years-ago-today.

16. "Mobile Fact Sheet," Pew Research Center, February 5, 2018, accessed
November 27, 2018, http://www.pewinternet.org/fact-sheet/mobile/.

17. Anton Troianovski, "Cellphones Are Eating the Family Budget," *Wall
Street Journal*, September 28, 2012, https://www.wsj.com/articles/SB1
0000872396390444083304578018731890309450.

18. DavisFinancial, "I'm in debt up to my eyeballs . . . ," filmed February 2011, YouTube, video, 0:35, https://www.youtube.com/watch?v =r0HX4a5P8eE.

CHAPTER 6: MAKING PEACE WITH LOST TIME

1. Laura A. King, "The Health Benefits of Writing About Life Goals," *Personality and Social Psychology Bulletin* 27 (2001): 798–807.
2. Barry Schwartz, *The Paradox of Choice: Why More Is Less* (New York: Ecco, 2004), 22.

CHAPTER 8: THE POWER OF A POSITIVE PESSIMIST

1. "Optimism and Your Health," Harvard Health Publishing, May 2008, https://www.health.harvard.edu/heart-health/optimism-and -your-health; "Positive Thinking: Stop Negative Self-Talk to Reduce Stress," Mayo Clinic, https://www.mayoclinic.org/healthy-lifestyle /stress-management/in-depth/positive-thinking/art-20043950; Ciro Conversano, Alessandro Rotondo, Elena Lensi, Olivia Della Vista, Francesca Arpone, and Mario Antonio Reda, "Optimism and Its Impact on Mental and Physical Well-Being," NCBI, https://www .ncbi.nlm.nih.gov/pmc/articles/PMC2894461/.
2. M. E. P. Seligman, *Learned Optimism: How to Change Your Mind and Your Life* (New York: Vintage Books, 2006), 49–51.
3. J. K. Norem and N. Cantor, "Defensive Pessimism: Harnessing Anxiety as Motivation," *Journal of Personality and Social Psychology* 51, no. 6 (December 1986): 1208–17.

CHAPTER 10: PRESS PAUSE

1. Phillipe R. Goldin and James J. Gross, "Effects of Mindfulness-Based Stress Reduction (MBSR) on Emotion Regulation in Social Anxiety Disorder," *Emotion* 10, no. 1 (2010): 83–91, http://dx.doi.org/10.1037 /a0018441.
2. Goldin and Gross, "Effects of Mindfulness-Based Stress Reduction (MBSR) on Emotion Regulation," 83–91.

3. Kelly McGonigal, *The Willpower Instinct: How Self-Control Works, Why It Matters, and What You Can Do to Get More of It* (New York: Avery/Penguin Group USA, 2012).

4. Matthew T. Gailliot, Roy F. Baumeister, C. Nathan DeWall, Jon K. Maner, E. Ashby Plant, Dianne M. Tice, Lauren E. Brewer, and Brandon J. Schmeichel, "Self-Control Relies on Glucose as a Limited Energy Source: Willpower Is More Than a Metaphor," *Journal of Personality and Social Psychology* 92, no. 2 (2007): 325–36.

5. Kelly McGonigal, "Stress, Sugar and Self-Control," *Psychology Today*, November 21, 2011, https://www.psychologytoday.com/us/blog /the-science-willpower/201111/stress-sugar-and-self-control.

6. Dianne M. Tice, Roy F. Baumeister, Dikla Shmueli, and Mark Muraven, "Restoring the Self: Positive Affect Helps Improve Self-Regulation Following Ego Depletion," *Journal of Experimental Social Psychology* 43, no. 3 (2007): 379–84.

CHAPTER 11: THE TEMPERAMENT
TO EXPERIMENT

1. H. Takeuchi, Y. Taki, H. Hashizume, Y. Sassa, T. Nagase, R. Nouchi, and R. Kawashima, "Failing to Deactivate: The Association Between Brain Activity During a Working Memory Task and Creativity," *Neuroimage* 55, no. 2 (2011): 681–87, DOI: 10.1016/j.neuroimage .2010.11.052.

2. Lulu Xie, Hongyi Kang, Qiwu Xu, Michael J. Chen, Yonghong Liao, Meenakshisundaram Thiyagarajan, John O'Donnell, Daniel J. Christensen, Charles Nicholson, Jeffrey J. Iliff, Takahiro Takano, Rashid Deane, and Maiken Nedergaard, "Sleep Initiated Fluid Flux Drives Metabolite Clearance from the Adult Brain," *Science* 342, no. 6156 (2013): 373–77, DOI: 10.1126/science.1241224.

3. Robert Stickgold and Jeffrey M. Ellenbogen, "Sleep on It: How Snoozing Makes You Smarter," *Scientific American Mind*, accessed September 23, 2009, http://www. scientificamerican.com/article. cfm?id=how-snoozing-makesyou-smarter.

4. Cheryl Conner, "Fifty Essential Mobile Marketing Facts," *Forbes*,

November 12, 2013, https://www.forbes.com/sites/cherylsnappconner /2013/11/12/fifty-essential-mobile-marketing-facts/#7d6193917475.

5. Heather Mason Kiefer, "Empty Seats: Fewer Families Eat Together," Gallup, January 20, 2004, accessed November 27, 2018, https://news .gallup.com/poll/10336/empty-seats-fewer-families-eat-together.aspx.

ABOUT THE AUTHOR

V ALORIE BURTON helps readers find joy and resilience while navigating the challenges of modern life. She has written a dozen books on personal development and is founder of the Coaching and Positive Psychology (CaPP) Institute, which provides coaching, resilience training, and certification programs for individuals and organizations. Her unique combination of research, faith, and personal transparency inspires action and delivers practical tools to find fulfillment and purpose in work and life. She and her husband live near Atlanta, Georgia, with their children. Visit her at www.valorieburton.com and www.cappinstitute.com.